RUDE
DUDE's

BOOK OF FOOD

RUDE DUDE'S

BOOK OF FOOD

STORIES BEHIND SOME OF

THE CRAZY-COOL STUFF WE EAT

BY

RUDE DUDE

(TIM J. MYERS)

ILLUSTRATED BY JESS SMART SMILEY

Copyright © 2014 by Tim J. Myers
Illustrations © 2014 Jess Smart Smiley

Published by Familius LLC, www.familius.com

Familius books are available at special discounts for bulk purchases for sales
promotions, family, or corporate use. Special editions, including personalized
covers, excerpts of existing books, or books with corporate logos, can be created
in large quantities for special needs. For more information, contact Premium
Sales at 559-876-2170 or email specialmarkets@familius.com

Library of Congress Catalog-in-Publication Data

2014944033

pISBN 978-1-939629-21-0
eISBN 978-1-939629-61-6

Printed in the United States of America

Edited by Brooke Jorden
Cover Design by David Miles
Book Design by Maggie Wickes and David Miles

10 9 8 7 6 5 4 3 2 1

First Edition

CONTENTS

WARNING

This book will probably make you very,
very hungry!
Good luck with that.

Acknowledgements

Writers know more than most people do that "it takes a village" in every sense of the phrase. Research means tapping into the experience and expertise of others, usually strangers—taking precious things, as it were, out of their lives and labors. It's such an enrichment that I sometimes feel like a thief. And I never take it for granted.

So I want to thank the many authors and experts whose print or online works I consulted, or whom I spoke to either in person or via email. (I'm continually amazed at how generous people are with their knowledge!)

I especially want to thank the following individuals for their research and/or for their reading of the manuscript and endorsements of it: Dr. Yasuko Nakamachi; Jennifer 8. Lee; Chef Jimmy Canora of Delmonico's; Dr. Marjorie Freedman of San Jose State University; Dr. Louis E. Grivetti, Professor Emeritus at the University of California-Davis; and Dr. Katharine Heintz, Dr. Barbara Burns, Dr. Christina Ri, and Dr. Lisa Kealhofer, all of my own Santa Clara University. These are some amazing people!

I also want to particularly thank the wonderful people at Sneha's Restaurant in Sunnyvale, California, and all the restaurant people who've ever fed me and my family. The giving of food is,

I think, a deeply good and human thing, and those who prepare and serve food to others are doing something beautiful to make the world a better place. I'm filled with gratitude toward them.

And finally, I have to thank my family for the immeasurable fun, knowledge, and love we've shared over our decades of taking meals together.

Tim J. Myers

Santa Clara

2014

CHAPTER 1

HEY, RUDE DUDE—WHY'D YOU WRITE THIS BOOK?

Yo, people!

Rude Dude here. Hope you're doin' great and feelin' good and your feet don't itch. (Actually, I put that in because my left foot just started itching. Ahh—I scratched—that's better.)

I also hope you're not crazy-hungry, since you're kids and you probably sometimes feel like you could eat a horse and all that. Except, please— leave the horses alone!

The thing is, I can't really tell if you're hungry or not, because I'm here and you're there. Maybe if I was there I could tell—because

you'd have that hungry look that makes your eyes scrunch up and your mouth get all frowny. Or I'd hear your stomachs growling like a dog who just spotted the mailman. Or you'd be all, "Rude Dude, we're STARVING!" You know, like baby birds chirping with their beaks open. Only I don't think you'd be asking for worms and bugs. Well—maybe you're THAT hungry.

Anyhoo—if you ARE hungry, I hope you get fed soon. If you're not, don't worry; by the time you will be. Because it's all about FOOD, dudes!

But you probably figured that out from the title, huh?

Okay—here's the deal. Rude Dude understands that sometimes history seems boring. But I swear to you on my Eternal Love of Pizza: history is very, VERY cool! If it seems boring, that's probably because you're not getting the whole story.

Because, dudes, that's what history really is—a story. In fact, it's THE story of everything and everybody! And there's nothing cooler than stories—you know it, I know it, and the babies in their strollers know it.

Let me give you an example—just a teenie-weenie one out of all the awesome stories that make up the Big Story of history. This one isn't about food—but it's about water.

Maybe you've heard of Alexander the Great; maybe you haven't. But he was as real as you or me. He lived in Macedonia long ago, a king's son, and he conquered most of the known world. You know, got together a big army and took over different countries—from Greece all the way to India. (And this was at a time when the only thing faster than your own two feet was a horse!)

Okay, two things right off. First, Rude Dude thinks conquering is very uncool—but some people back then thought it was a good thing to do. Second, maybe you think even this story's boring. "OK," you might be saying, "so dusty old Alexander was a hotshot conqueror guy. Big snooze."

But just let me tell you a bit of the story. Here's how I heard it.

He and his army were crossing this huge, baking-hot desert in Central Asia, and they'd almost run out of water. The soldiers had none left, and they were suffering—bad. At one point, Alexander called a halt, and one of his servants came running up with some of the last water, carrying it in Alexander's helmet. The servant bowed and offered the water to his lord.

Alexander turned around, looked at all his parched and dusty men, then lifted the helmet . . . and poured the water out on the sand.

He didn't say a word, but they understood: he wouldn't drink till they all did.

Pretty cool, right? Like I said: history is stories. And even something as ordinary-seeming as food has lots of great stories that go along with it!

A cool little thing happened to me the other day. I was putting this empty bag of ravioli in the recycling bin when I noticed the picture on the front. You know, the kind of picture they put on grocery stuff to show what's inside and how yum-alicious it is. Since this was ravioli, it showed things like white cheese, tomatoes, and garlic. And that made me think of water buffalo and poison and World War II . . .

Do I sound crazy? Well, maybe I am—a little. But that's not why I thought of these cool things. They popped into my head because they're part of the amazing story of pasta (which you'll hear about later).

Believe me, dudes—the history of food is just one bangin' story after another!

Even the basic stuff is cool. Millions of years ago, the continents split apart from each other. Then they each ran off in a different

KEEP BEING AWESOME

31 million Americans skip breakfast—yikes! That's not only a lot of cereal or scrambled eggs going uneaten, but it's bad for people! Think about it. The longest time you go without food is overnight, and breakfast is fuel for all the things you do till lunch. So don't forget to do some chompin' in the a.m.!

direction like someone had just set off a stink bomb. Because of that, plants on the separate continents started evolving differently. Animals, too. So different kinds of food developed, separated by oceans. And of course, different people invented all kinds of different ways of preparing all this different stuff.

But when people started sailing those oceans and "discovering" other countries, the whole thing reversed. Today, we live in a world where different foods have spread all over the place! Wheat started in Europe, but now American farmers grow tons of it. Coffee began in Africa, but it's now a major crop in Brazil, Java, and Jamaica. Rice is from Asia, but Texas and California now produce famous kinds of it. Peanuts and chocolate—both from the Americas—are now big in West Africa. Chili peppers are famous in spicy Asian foods, and Ireland loves potatoes—both of which came from South America. It's just a big giant mash-up! (Hey—a little potato pun there! And it happened purely by accident!)

I learned something else while writing this book, too: the foods I love most tend to be the super-popular ones that started in one place and are now eaten all over the planet. Lots of us love stuff we think comes from our own country, so we'd be surprised to find out that . . . it really doesn't!

Consider Kit Kats. I thought they were as American as apple pie—which, by the way, is English, not American. Kit Kat bars are the same. Don't believe me? Look at the wrapper—they were first made in York, a city in northern England. (Of course apple pie can't be American because apples didn't grow in America till Europeans brought them over—and they first grew in Kazakhstan, in Asia!)

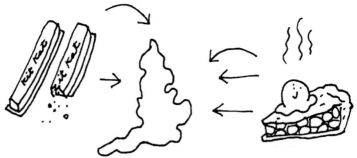

This idea of stuff spreading all over the world—the Dude happens to like it. A lot. Because most of the time it makes the world better. And it shows that, despite all the differences among people, we're still a lot alike. Have you heard how chimpanzees are 98 percent the same as human beings in their genes? ("Genes," not "jeans"! Don't be dopey, dudes—you know chimps don't wear pants! Though, I suppose if they went to the mall, they'd head straight for Banana Republic.)

Well, it's even more true when you compare humans to other humans—we're the same species, after all! Even though we often SEEM completely different, we have a lot in common. Maybe that's why certain foods appeal to millions, even billions of people. Lots of us, for example, will see chocolate and say, "Okie-dokie, Smokey!"

Oh, and one more thing. History just keeps on changing, and food history does, too. Stuff is happening now that'll show up in the history books of the future. One of the big deals these days is that we're learning a lot more about how food affects our bodies. I love burgers and pizza and great chow like that—but I'm

KEEP BEING AWESOME

How would you feel if somebody dumped 52 pounds of something on your head? That's a lot of something, huh? Well, one can of regular soda has 10 teaspoons of sugar in it—and your average American person knocks back 500 cans a year. So skip the sugary soda and you're skipping 52 POUNDS OF SUGAR A YEAR. But don't worry—there's always your birthday cake!

HELP!

also careful about what I eat. I don't eat TOO MUCH pizza or chocolate, and I make sure I get plenty of fruits, vegetables, and all the healthy stuff—you know, like on the My-Plate diagram (www.choosemyplate.gov). And I exercise and play games all the time. Because as much as I love burgers and pizza, I love hiking, biking, and basketball even more.

But more on all that later.

So why'd I write this book? Because the story of food is down-right fascinating! And I think you're gonna love it, too. Not to mention that, as they say when they offer you brussels sprouts, this stuff is GOOD FOR YOU. It may make you a better eater and a better citizen of the world, but it's DEFINITELY going to be FUN!

Alrighty then. Sit back, buckle up, and fix your chin-strap: Rude Dude's taking you on a wild ride through the world of food. I guarantee your mouth will soon be watering!

Peace out. Word to your mother.

Yours awesomely,

R. D.

P.S. Oh, and dudes—you may notice that I write things in this book like "gonna" and such, with plenty of slang, too. Maybe you want to ask, "If the Dude can write like that, why can't we?" Well, the answer is, you can—IF you're writing a character (which is what Rude Dude is). The Dude loves to write; he changes what he writes depending on who he's writing to and what he's writing about. But he knows all the rules and how to use them! Learning to write Standard English is good for you—ya heard?!

Language is power, dudes, so learn your stuff—it's worth it!

P.P.S. Oh, and calling myself "Rude Dude"? Hey, I'm not really impolite—just a little nutsy. Quite goof-tacular, in fact.

CHOCOLATE

CHAPTER 2

Choc Rocks

Alright, cats and kittens, let's talk about something SO delicious even modern science calls it *Theobroma*—"Food of the Gods." We just call it chocolate.

And luckily, the gods seem OK with us eating it. Because when I think about chocolate, all I can say is—whoa.

And I'm not the only one. Chocolate is one of the best-loved foods on Earth. In 1998, for example, Americans alone ate 3.3 billion pounds—that's BILLIONS, Uncle Scrooge! Americans buy one billion dollars' worth of chocolate every Valentine's Day—I kid you not! Nine out of ten people like chocolate (and some say the tenth is probably lying). There's even a group of chocolate-lovers called "Chocoholics Unanimous" (Get it? Instead of "anonymous"?) Sometimes I think I could go off "chocolateering"—you know, like a pirate, also known as a "buccaneer." I'd rig out a ship and steal other people's chocolate. But I couldn't have a crew—I wouldn't want to share.

But while I tell you about chocolate, I'll tell another story, too—a smaller but, to me, equally important one. Pay attention—there will be a quiz.

Once upon a time, there was this kid named Chocolate who stayed in his house all the time. He thought he was too pure to mix with anything else. So he just hung out, looking in the mirror or watching the Food Network. . . .

OK, more on that later. Now, about the very cool history of chocolate.

Chocolate historians have tracked the story down. (What—you think being a "chocolate histori-an" is weird? Beats being a bean-dip historian, if you ask me.) For thousands of years, wild cacao trees were growing in the jungles of what's now Vene-zuela. (It's pronounced "kuh-KOW"—sounds like a little explosion, right?) Cacao trees grow these pineapple-sized pods right from their trunks and branches— and people learned early on how to open them, get the beans out, then roast and grind the beans. Humans have been growing cacao for at least 3000 years.

Chocolate back then tasted bitter. Still, the love of cacao spread to the Olmec people of Central America, then the Maya, then the Aztecs. People mixed it in water, hot or cold, adding things like vanilla, cinnamon, pepper, or chilies—a long way from our hot cocoa with whipped cream! (The Maya would add corn for extra calories before going to war.) And "chocolate" meant liquid; nobody'd even dreamed of making chocolate for eating. So sad!

The Aztecs even used cacao beans for money. (I'm glad we don't; I'd eat my change before I could spend it.) They believed chocolate was consumed by 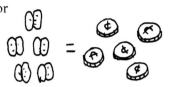 the gods in Paradise, so they also drank it during their religious ceremonies (wish we followed that custom!). Moctezuma II, Aztec Emperor when the Spanish first came to Mexico, is said to have taken fifty shots a day, in solid-gold cups. Though he probably didn't drink them all—I hate to think what that much chocolate would do to someone's digestion. (And check it out: After Cortez, the Spaniard who conquered the Aztecs, went back to Spain, he always kept a full pot of chocolate on his writing table.) The Aztecs even made human sacrifices to the goddesses involved with chocolate—and what do you think they gave the victims as a last meal? Yep. Chocolate. So we can probably conclude that they died happy . . . ?

OK—back to our little story:

So Chocolate stays inside all the time. (Which would drive me BONKERS! But then, I'm not a food. Though maybe to lions or whatever. . . .) But Chocolate starts getting bored. One day his parents say, "You know, you could step outside now and then—you won't melt!" (Well, actually . . .)

OK. Back to history.

At first, Europeans didn't realize what chocolate could be—poor guys! Columbus saw cacao beans in 1503, but he didn't have a clue. (No surprise—dude thought he was in India!) They say that in 1579, some English pirates captured a ship full of cacao beans, but thought it was sheep droppings—so they burned it! A Spanish priest in Peru called chocolate "loathsome" and "scum." These mixed-up tourists just didn't get it! Cortez tasted "cacahuatl," as the Aztecs called it, and set up plantations to grow it—but mainly just to make money. Literally. Growing your own money is pretty cool (despite how people say it doesn't grow on trees)—but he really missed the boat on chocolate as a drink, at least for a while.

But he didn't miss the boat back to Spain, and soon foamy chocolate was the style among Spanish royalty. For a century, Spain seems to have kept chocolate secret. Around this time, something happened that set chocolate on the path to world fame.

The thing is, humans have this funny tendency: we like to mix all kinds of different stuff together. Someone—we don't really know who, though legend says it was some monks—decided against chili and added something to their cacao beans that just, well, really clicked:

Sugar.

Which, by the way, was also an expensive and "foreign" food from the New World.

OK, choc crocs (that means you people who total-ly chomp chocolate)—more on our little story:

Chocolate finally left his house. There he was, walk-ing down the street. "I'll go downtown," he told himself, "so everyone can admire my purity." But at the same moment, on the other side of town, another dude was leaving his house. He decided to go downtown, too . . .

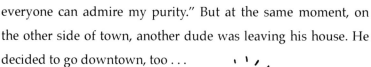

Is the suspense killing you yet? Not much longer now. A little more history first, though.

Now when chocolate turned sweet—and when the secret got out of Spain—it basically took off across Europe. And why not, right? Marie Antoinette, the queen who got her head chopped off during the French Revolution, also lost her head for chocolate—she had her own "chocolatier" to make it for her, with stuff like orchids, orange blossoms, and almonds mixed in. Soon "chocolate houses" were a huge fad; the first one opened in London in 1657. (No, not houses made of chocolate, you brainless choc crocs! They were like coffee houses.)

Then an English doctor named Sir Hans Sloane added something else great: cow's milk. And that, kids, is how chocolate milk was born. Maybe we should call Sloane the Choc Doc. He also started the amazing British Museum—but I'm not sure which of these two ideas was the coolest.

Now, more on our story.

So there's Chocolate just trucking along. It's a warm day; he's starting to feel soft. But he figures it's no big deal. On the other side of town, Mystery Dude is also strutting along thinking how great he is (which he is) . . .

So close! But back to history again.

Chocolate was still really expensive, though. And not just money-wise. There are horrible, sad parts to the story, too. Because everybody loved it so much, Europeans set up chocolate plantations in tropical countries like Mexico and Brazil—and some of their workers were slaves. At first these were natives of those tropical countries. But when many of them died from European diseases, landowners started buying Africans. And although cacao farming is no longer done by slaves, it's important of course that people in such jobs are paid fairly for their work and have decent working conditions. And that isn't always the case.

But there's happy news as well. Over time, chocolate got much cheaper—and even tastier!

We don't know for sure who made the first solid chocolate. I've seen one book that says Spaniards made solid chocolate rolls and cakes back in 1674. The Frys, an English family, say they sold the first chocolate for eating in 1846. (Shouldn't we have a holiday for that or something?) Even then, though, chocolate was rough and grainy. But during the Industrial Revolution (basically the late 1700s to the early 1800s) and afterwards, experts learned to make it smoother, creamier, even moldable—so we can have things like chocolate Easter Bunnies. (On Valentine's Day in Japan, I once got a small chocolate motorcycle and a chocolate pistol; I ate the pistol first, just to be safe). And then, around 1900, the prices of cacao and sugar dropped really low.

Oh, am I boring you? Does all this talk about inventions and prices leave you cold? Well, think about it, dudes—when you're craving a candy bar,

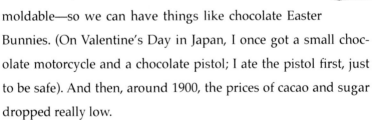

KEEP BEING AWESOME

The thing is—your body was made to move! So get out there and walk or run or play or swim or bike or anything else that puts you in motion on your own. Pick things that are fun to do. Take the stairs instead of the elevator. Exercise is INCREDIBLY good for you!

you can usually scratch that itch pretty fast. But all kinds of stuff had to happen in history or else you couldn't! Before World War I, most people only got chocolate at Christmas or on their birthdays. Bummer! Is that the kind of world you want to live in?!

I didn't think so.

Back to our little story:

Chocolate's walking down First Street. Mystery Dude's walking down First Avenue. Neither is paying attention to where he's going. Closer, closer—both heading toward the same corner, on the same side of the street....

But I can't tell you the ending yet. Let's get back to the history, shall we?

As chocolate got cheaper and better, there was a chocolate explosion. (Well, not literally—sorry!). The love of chocolate spread across the globe.

Not everybody's nuts about it, of course. In much of Africa, for example, it's not super popular—which may have something to do with African heat and the fact that chocolate melts at about 93 degrees (in other words, "melts in your mouth"—we're all about 98.6, remember?). And sometimes chocolate's worth so much that people sell it rather than eat it—they need the money.

But overall chocolate tends to bring the world together. And people can get pretty intense about it. Some examples:

- How many festivals are held for, say, green beans? Not many. But I know of at least seven chocolate festivals in my part of the country alone—just in February! And they have them all over the United States. There's "Chocolate Week" in New York City, "Feast of Chocolate" in Carson City, Nevada, "Chocolate Lovers Fling" in Boulder, Colorado—you get the picture. (Hey! Why not a Chocolate and Green Bean Festival? That'd be funky . . .)

- By 1930, forty thousand different kinds of chocolate candy bars existed. So hurry up and make your choice already!

- If you've got sixty bucks, you can buy a chocolate waterfall machine; it sits on a table pumping melted chocolate like a fountain down over three ledges. You dip stuff like fruit and cookies in the flow. I'm not making this up.

- The biggest chocolate bar ever made was an Italian monstrosity that weighed over 5,000 pounds. (That's one monster I'd LIKE to meet!).

- The most expensive chocolate I've heard about goes for $2,600—a pound! It has French truffles in it, a special and expensive kind of mushroom. But holy moneybags—that's quite a chunk of change!

My favorite "chocolate insanity" story, though, comes from a book published in 1656. Thomas Gage tells how Mexican-Indian women of that time would drink chocolate during church, since the Catholic rule was that you couldn't eat anything for three hours before the service. The bishop tried to stop the chocolate drinking—he thought it was cheating (and he had a point!) But he turned up dead—some say from poisoned chocolate the women sent him! The whole disagreement was so important the Pope himself finally declared that "liquids" (which included chocolate) didn't "break the fast," so people could go on drinking it. Surprise, surprise.

And here's a fun fact: In Japan, Valentine's Day is different. The girls give chocolate to the boys. Whoa—maybe I should move there.

Alright—we've arrived at the climax of our little tale:

Suddenly—WHAM! Chocolate and Mystery Dude crash right into each other! And because it's hot out, and they're both so soft—they just kind of mush all together . . .

But this isn't sad—it's stupendous! Because Mystery Dude is . . .

Can you guess?

I'll give you some hints:

Chocolate and Mystery Dude have been deliciously together since 1922.

A guy named Reese was the first one to mix them.

And together they make one of the best-selling candy "bars" of all time!

Give up?

Mystery Dude is PEANUT BUTTER. And the mystery candy is the peanut butter cup!

Which is IMPORTANT, people! For one thing, it's Rude Dude's favorite. But it also shows what can happen when human beings put different things together in new ways. I mean, you gotta feel sorry for those people who lived before 1922!

Imagine if Moctezuma could taste a peanut butter cup. If he'd had those, he probably wouldn't have needed fifty cups of chocolate a day, huh?

And of course, this just shows (again) how much people love chocolate.

So choc on, amigos!

Quiz:

When you become a gazillionaire someday and want to thank Rude Dude for all the wonderful things he's done, what are you going to send him five boxcars full of?

(The answer is at the back of the book. Hint: It's not just plain chocolate!)

A Poem for Dessert

ODE TO PEANUT BUTTER

There's some that says it's lumpy—
let 'em grump.
There's them what says it's sticky—
like it's icky! It ain't tricky if you know
how the lovely stuff should go
all tasteful, good, and greedy down your gullet.
I'll bet a silver dollar
that, like as not, it hits the spot
if you know how to swaller.

Oh Lord, You have created
many things, both small and great, and
lots of what You made has done elated us just fine.
You made skies and pies, and ants and pants,
and trains a-chugging choo choo;
the blazing sun, the deepy sea, the parrot, pig and monkey—
But the best thing that You gave us,
delish enough to save us,
was peanut butter, whether smooth or
chunky.

So children, mind your peanut butter—
eat it, treat it right.
It suits me fine if you should hug the jar
in bed at night.
There ain't but just a few things in this
world,
boys and girls, so deserving
of all your love and all your loyal serving
as these three:

Your country, with its flag that flaps and flutters—
your own and onliest dear old darling mother—
and your peanut butter.

CHAPTER 3

A Short History of the World

(from a Hamburger-Lover's Point of View)

Dude, these are amazing times—you know it, I know it, and the babies in their strollers know it. But historians a thousand years from now won't talk about computers or space shuttles or cable TV. They'll call our time the Age of the Hamburger. Because it's for dang sure that the hamburger is one of the coolest things to happen in the last couple centuries.

The average American eats three burgers

a week. I guess that makes me two or three average Americans. I'm like, run a burger up the flagpole and I'll salute. Then I'll climb up after it. Gajillions of people feel the same. Hamburgers appear on American menus more than any other food. There was even a French chef in the White House—French, I'm saying, the gourmets of the world—who specialized in milk shakes and hamburgers. And at any time, one out of three Americans has downed a burger in the past 24 hours. I've read that all the burgers McDonald's has sold add up to 16 for every person on the planet today.

Wicked lot of ground beef, huh?

As you might expect, the popularity of hamburgers is causing some problems, too. I'll talk about that in the final chapter. For now, let's just see how the whole thing happened.

I figure the sacred evolution of the hamburger began back when ancient cave-people knocked animals on the head with clubs and became meat-eaters. And somewhere along the line, some all-thumbs guy dropped his zebra haunch in the fire. Then he started crying and blubbering, then was dumb enough to snatch it out. Naturally, he burned his fingers and stuck them in his mouth to cool them off—and realized his fingertips tasted really, really delicious. (Let's hope he didn't get confused and accidentally invent cannibalism.) So people learned to cook their meat.

Another good thing was when civilized people (which means people who thought they were cooler and smarter than cave-people) figured out you could take a bunch of wheat and pound the crud out of it and make flour, then bread. Which was pretty awesome—only they didn't have a clue about hamburger buns yet.

So time went by, and we had the Middle Ages in Europe, and the Chinese invented paper and gunpowder, and Africa had some big kingdoms—you know, the usual. But then something amazing happened: the Mongols invented steak tartare. (Well, cows had something to do with it, too).

SQUISH!

The Mongols, believe it or not, would stick raw meat under their saddles, then ride all over the place and fight and stuff, and that would make the meat tender. I know—way gross! (I notice nobody says much about how the meat smelled). But some experts say other people had ground their beef centuries before those grouchy Mongol guys flavored theirs with saddle-smell and horse sweat. I'll bet you good green money it was some ancient Egyptian or Babylonian kid, poking at his dinner—and before his ancient mom could say "Don't play with your food," he'd poked his meat till it was basically ground beef. Genius!

Anyway, the deal is, when the Mongols took over Russia, they not only brought, like, death and destruction, but Russians and

Finns really flipped over their style of meat. Which I don't get. But maybe back then, sweat-and-saddle flavor was like teriyaki or cool ranch to us. This kind of meat came to be called "steak tartare," after the Mongols. ("Tartar" is another name for Mongols. Weird, huh? I mean, do I go around saying my name is Tim but also Freddie?)

Eventually steak tartare came to mean raw beef that was all chopped up—that's basically what "ground beef" means (though, later on, people started cooking it). And that made it easier and faster for busy people to eat. And people liked that. So it spread, and trader guys from Germany took the recipe back to their country, and when Germans came to America, they brought along steak tartare.

KEEP BEING AWESOME

Of all the stuff you eat every day, half of it should be fruits and vegetables. Which is very monkey-like and cool, if you ask me. And since we humans are very monkey-like and cool, it's a perfect match!

But the whole name thing gets even more complicated here, and funny. Because Americans started calling it a "hamburger"—which means a person who lives in Hamburg, Germany, which is apparently the city it came from. (Hamburg has a big port, and lots of Germans, especially in the 1850s, headed for America by boarding ships there.) There are a couple of weird things about this, in my opinion.

First, you won't believe it—but Americans also eat something else named after a German city. I mean, what are the chances? One particular country across an ocean goes crazy over two different foods—both of which are meat—both of which become sandwiches—both of which take a special bun—and each of which is named for a German city. Hot dogs were originally called "frankfurters," from the city of Frankfurt. "Frankfurter" means a person from that city (which actually allows you, if you go to Germany, to pull out a hot dog and say, in front of your parents, "Look at the buns on that frankfurter"—and not get in trouble for being impolite).

But even weirder: In Germany, they later started calling the hamburger "American steak." Holy rump roast! THEY gave us the hamburger—we named if after them—and now they've named it after us!

(Which makes me think: You know that dog we call the "German shepherd"? Do you suppose Germans call it the "American sheepen-vatcher" or something like that? Just wondering.)

We know that in 1867, a doctor named James H. Salisbury said that raw beef was bad for people, and then suggested scraping the beef and pressing it into patties. So that was a BIG step. And cool enough that people started calling the dish "Salisbury steak" after the doctor. People ate it on a plate with a knife and fork, which is super-fancy compared to the Mongols and (luckily) 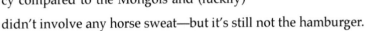 didn't involve any horse sweat—but it's still not the hamburger.

We also know that the famous New York restaurant Delmonico's had on its menu—back in 1834—a dish called "Hamburg steak." Now this wasn't a burger either—it was bunless. (Sure glad I'm not—how would I sit?) But it's another step along the road to our beloved United States of Burgermania.

And just in case you read somewhere that the story is fake, get this: I emailed Delmonico's, and this wonderful guy named Chef Jimmy Canora emailed me back, explaining the evidence that means the story is true. This is a pretty big deal for the people at Delmonico's—how would YOU feel if your great-great-great Grandpa Geezer served something burger-ish way, way back when, even if he didn't know a bun from a popgun? You'd be proud, right? So are they. (That's why, if you ever run into Chef Jimmy from Delmonico's, you should tell him we all think he's a Major Dude). By the way, back then, a whole fancy-restaurant meal of Hamburg steak cost . . . 10 cents. Whoa! But this form of beef was sold even cheaper in other places, so that made it popular, too.

And we know that in 1876, there was a huge fair and "exposition" in Philadelphia—and that a man named Philip Jauber ran a big German restaurant there, one that could serve 1200 customers at once—lots of whom ate Hamburg steak, loved it, then talked about it. (Which is pretty much what I'm doing right now.)

MINE!

But after that, things get sketchy. Because in America, everybody and his cousin and his pet turtle claims they invented the hamburger. The thing is, it's not a burger till you put a ground-beef pattie between two pieces of bread. (A "pattie"? What's up with that? Can you imagine calling it a "betty" or a "sue"?) And the fact is, of all the people who SAY they invented burgers, none have real proof. So it's like when there's a bunch of little kids and somebody burps but no one will fess up: we know it happened, but we don't know who did it.

You always hear that this rich English lord, the Earl of Sandwich, was busy playing cards and asked his cook to put meat between two pieces of bread, which was the first sandwich. (Luckily they didn't call it an "earl"—but then, that would have gone nicely with "pattie." Earl and Pattie—kinda romantic.) And that's true, though it may be that this particular guy wasn't actually the first one to figure that out. Of course, there wouldn't be hamburgers if somebody hadn't invented the sandwich first.

But apparently it took a super-brain to make a sandwich out of ground beef. And whoever did that is, in my carnivorous opinion, the Golden Hero of Human Culture.

But then something else happened to make hamburgers super-popular: lunch wagons. Lots of Americans worked in factories or similar places. A guy named Walter Scott got the idea to sell food out of a wagon near a factory in Providence, Rhode Island. Then a guy named Ruel B. Jones—which is a very cool name—made an even bigger wagon. And people loved grabbing a burger, on the cheap, at these places—so a good idea, as always, started spreading. The "hamburger steak sandwich" was becoming a star. Soon, it showed up in restaurants, then in cookbooks. Eva Greene Fuller had hamburgers in her *The Up-to-Date Sandwich Book* in 1927, for example—but when the book was published in England, the editors took out all the hamburger recipes!

Hey, England! Bet you're sorry about that now!

Hamburgers were on their

way to becoming one of the great American foods. It's too bad that, in the early days, some evil dudes would mix in chopped dog, cat, or rat meat. In fact, other business people decided to show just how clean their hamburger restaurants could be; maybe they heard about the Mongols, eh? So they painted their places all white and filled them with gleaming, stainless-steel equipment—and made tons of money. The first hamburger chain restaurants appeared in the 1920s, White Castle being the most famous.

Then came the 50s, the time when the car just about took over America. At that point, an even bigger change came to hamburgers, and it happened the way lots of cultural change happens: somebody combined one thing with something else, and the two just clicked. And although it may not sound very appetizing, the two things were cars and burgers.

What I mean is that millions of Americans now lived in suburbs instead of cities and got around by driving instead of walking or taking streetcars. So these two guys named McDonald—hmm, getting any hints here?—opened a burger place near Pasadena, California, in 1937. They set the place up like an assembly line for making burgers. But after a while, a sharp businessman named Ray Croc came along, bought the company, and started opening up new McDonald's joints all over the place. And McDonald's just took off—it got more and more popular, made more and more hamburgers, made more and more money, and then spread all over the world. In Japan, the restaurant is called "Makudo-narudo"—and many Japanese kids are so used to it they think it's Japanese!

KEEP BEING AWESOME

One-fourth of what you eat every day should be whole grains—like bread, pasta, and rice. But here's the thing: the whole-grain (brown) versions are best, since they contain more Vitamin B, E, and fiber than white bread, white pasta, or white rice. Brown is beauful, baby!

So now we live in this glorious and somewhat ketchup-stained Age of the Hamburger. Which beats the Age of Knocking Animals on the Head and the Age of Eating Stuff Just Made from Flour—and, if you ask me, totally beats the Age of Eating Meat from Under Your Saddle.

The hamburger is like one of those American movie stars known all over the world. In Korea, you can get a kimchi burger, which includes that spicy cabbage dish, or even a "Burning Squid Burger." Dude! In the Philippines, some burgers come with steamed rice. India has burgers made of fresh cheese and walnuts or from dried peas; the McAloo Tikki Burger from McDonald's is the best-seller there. In

Pakistan, one kind of burger is made of lentils and lamb. Norwegian McDonald's restaurants offer the McLak, which is salmon. And plenty of countries have their own hamburger chains now.

The people at Mickey D's also figured out something else: if you get kids liking your restaurant, you'll make more money. So they came up with the Happy Meal and free toys and Ronald McDonald and all that stuff. Statistics show that 97 percent of American kids know who Ronald McDonald is—only Santa Claus is more widely recognized. And Jolly Old Saint Nick doesn't feed you! Don't forget, dudes: they're after you, too, and they know you'll bug your parents to get what you want.

You know the cereal aisle at the grocery story with all those colors and "a prize inside" and characters like Count Chocula? Hey, I think prizes and cartoons are awesome, too. But you shouldn't choose your cereal just for that stuff, especially if the cereal's too sugary or whatever. Dudes, when you're in the cereal aisle, you should feel a little like a fly around spider webs. The cereal makers want your parents' money! But more on that later.

Speaking of money, dig this: Hamburgers are now part of "haute cuisine," that is, super-fancy gourmet cooking. And that set off a kind of "war" to see who could sell the most expensive burger. This'll knock your socks off. (And if you're just wearing flip-flops, hold on to those, too.)

In 1975, New York's well-known Club 21 started selling a burger that cost $21. But that was nothing! Another New York restaurant went to $29—a Miami restaurant then bumped it to

$30—then a Las Vegas joint hit $50, and another went to $99. Not to be outdone, a London restaurant hit $104, a Spanish place hit $110, and a New Zealand-beef version sold for $134.

But this is all just chicken feed (well—I hope not!). Because back in Vegas, the Fleur de Lys offered a $5000 burger, complete with champagne. It even comes with a certificate to prove you bought it, kinda like those Cabbage Patch Dolls or NeoPets did. (I'm thinking the certificate proves you were a dope to spend so much money on a burger—but maybe that's just me.)

We haven't covered the whole story of the hamburger, though—there are sub-plots, too. Like some comedian says, imagine the first prehistoric guy who saw a wild cow—then told everybody, "I'm going over to that animal, and I'm gonna tug on that pink hangy-down part in the back, and whatever comes out, I'll just let it sit till it gets all hard—then I'll eat it." Because whoever that brave lad or lassie was, he or she invented cheese. But more on that later.

And then there's the milkshake, which became a natural option for the traditional burger-joint meal.

And what about Columbus?

"What?" you say. "Columbus helped, too?" Oh, heck yeah! Check it out: bumping into America was pretty important, I guess—but the big thing was that Europeans found something awesome in the New World they'd never seen before: potatoes. And if you don't respect the lowly but delicious spud—well, I just feel sorry for you. Think about it: what's a burger . . . without fries?

Now I have to throw in a part about how french fries aren't the healthiest food in the world. Because you can't eat 'em every day— you know it, I know it, and the babies in their strollers know it. On the other hand, a burger WITHOUT fries? To the Dude's way of thinking, that's just WRONG!

So, to sum up: The solar system condenses out of a humungous disk of dust and gas—Earth forms—people evolve—a bunch of other stuff happens—then we figure out how to make hamburgers and fries, which make people really, really happy—then Elvis sells a lot of records—and here we are today, in this beautiful world where American people eat almost five billion burgers a year. That's right, math-whiz—I said "billion." Lots of people around the world dig them, too.

By now, though, you may be thinking I'm some kind of burger-obsessed weirdo. But I'm just as sane as you are—maybe a little more. So I have to point out that, in all this whole ginormous world, one thing exists that's actually superior to hamburgers.

Dudes—can't you guess?

That's right: cheeseburgers.

To Learn More:

Would you like to learn more about the history of hamburgers? Then don't just sit there—get off your duff and do some research! And if you come across anything really cool, let me know, will ya?

A Poem for Dessert

PEANUTS AND COKE

(Dedicated to my sons Seth and Nick, who felt this way)

The stewardess brings us peanuts and coke!
The flight is long and we get bored,
our parents just lie back and snore—
but the stewardess brings us peanuts and coke!

We love the peanuts, the diet coke!
We're tired of Dad's old knock-knock jokes,
and airplane meals make us choke—
but the stewardess brings us peanuts and coke!

"There's more to life than peanuts and coke!"
our mother says; we know she's right,
but over the sea in the dark of night
we're waiting to get more peanuts and coke!

Peanuts and coke! Peanuts and coke!
Someone yelled that the wing is broke,
and yes, we both can smell the smoke,
but the stewardess brought us peanuts and coke!

CHAPTER 4

OODLES OF...
WHAT ELSE?

A w, come on—you already guessed it, right?

No? But you can rhyme, correcto? It can't be "oodles of poodles" (unless you're on a very strange diet). If you said "doodles"—well, those are awesome but, again, rather unsnarfable. (Except for Cheez Doodles—but that's different.) The real answer is more basic.

And if you use your _____, you'll realize that our topic today IS _____s.

noodles

Oodles of noodles. Get it? Go back and fill in the blanks if you didn't.

So why noodles? For one thing, they're one of the world's greatest foods. And there's something unique about them, at least in my book. (Hey, "in my book"—get it? The book you're reading right now!)

I love burgers, pizza, chocolate, all the rest—but noodles are the only food in this book that are more like a toy than food. You could try playing with a hamburger, but it wouldn't be much fun (and it's a bit disrespectful to cows, if you ask me.) But slurping noodles is cool! Or maybe you know that Italian trick where you twist a forkful of noodles into your spoon.

In China—which is basically Noodle Central—people have different styles of noodle-gnawing. Rolling them around your chopsticks is called "eating a drumstick," because it looks like a chicken leg (which looks like a drumstick—well, kind of. Don't try playing a drum with it). If you bite your noodles, you're acting like a cow; they

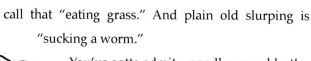

call that "eating grass." And plain old slurping is "sucking a worm."

You've gotta admit—noodles are a blast!

And dudes, they've been a blast for a long, LONG time. Recently, scientists in China found the world's oldest noodles. What kept the noodles from rotting away was a bowl—which a gigantic earthquake turned upside down over the noodles—which were then buried 10 feet deep by a terrible flood.

So how long ago do you guess this poor unfortunate person sat down to dinner, not knowing dessert would be an earthquake and a flood? Take a guess.

Try 4,000 years.

That means that human beings have, to date, consumed at least 4,000 years' worth—which is whole OCEANS of noodles. It also means that, though lots of countries claim to have invented noodles, we're pretty sure the Chinese were first. So these 4,000-year-old noodles are the coolest. I don't want to eat them; I don't dance with mummies, either. But it's awesome to know how long people have been slurping this delicious food.

And the Chinese are crazy for noodles. For example, they see noodles as a symbol of long life—since they're long, get it? (Because of this, it's unlucky to cut them; tell that to your parents when you feel like slurping.) Kids get "Birthday Noodles" instead of cake. People give pregnant women "Blessed Noodles," friends give friends "Peace Noodles," and old or sick people get "Health Noodles." Noodles are given after a child is born, and some Chinese leave fresh noodles at gravesites to honor their dead.

A guy named Shu Hsi, one of ancient China's smartest people, even wrote a poem called "A Rhapsody on Noodles." "Rhapsody" is when you're really, really into something, and you just go joyfully on and on about it. Other East Asians also love to get their noodle on; I've read that about 40 percent of all the flour in Asia is used to make . . . yep, noodles. Now that's popularity. (By the way—Shu Hsi's book also had recipes for cooking wolf, crane, swan, and snow leopard. And I've read a recipe from northwestern China for deep-fried camel's hump. Not exactly what you'd find at an American snack bar, huh?)

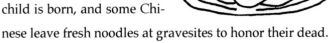

WHAT'S FOR DINNER?

But here's the thing: As noodle-nuts as Asia is, you'd think they had noodles from the beginning. But they didn't. As with pizza, it took a long time for the noodle to be invented.

KEEP BEING AWESOME

Protein foods should make up no more than one-fourth of your daily intake. Chicken, beans, fish, and nuts are best, and you should limit how much red meat or processed meat you eat. You know I love hamburgers—but I try not to eat too many!

Somewhere back in ancient times, people in China started grinding grains and made something brand new: flour, which became the main ingredient in a lot of different foods! So that was a big deal. Imagine how you'd feel if you lived on dried grasshoppers and somebody offered you a doughnut.

The Chinese first ground the grain called millet, and later rice and wheat, to make flour. Then they mixed water with the flour to make dough, and then steamed and boiled the dough. They made all kinds of stuff this way, in different shapes—dumplings, bread, buns, pancake-like things. And they called all this stuff "ping."

(Okay, I know what you're thinking—but this isn't the source of "ping-pong." That game was invented by the English, not the Chinese. The English word "ping-pong" comes from the sound of the ball hitting the paddle. And check it out! In England, they used to call the game "whiffwhaff." So don't get confused—ping-pong balls are NOT edible. Although, I'm not sure the babies in their strollers know that).

But where was I? Oh yeah. Once the Chinese started making "ping," we get the same wonderful old story: somebody comes up with something great, then somebody else makes it even better. And that "better" was noodles.

There are TONS of different ways to make Chinese noodles, and they're used in all kinds of dishes—from "Eight-Treasure Noodle" to "Chicken in a Lantern" (Holy moly! How'd that happen?) There's even one called "Ants Climbing a Tree," which is noodles with ant-like flecks of pork meat on them (which means YOU get to play anteater!).

So Chinese people, those lucky ducks, just went on eating noodles. But there's another part to that same wonderful old story, too—because when people in one place invent something great, that invention usually spreads to other places. And one place this new style spread to was good old Italy (which, as you'll learn from my pizza chapter, is a heavy-hitter when it comes to great food!).

Many people think noodles came to Italy from China, brought by the great traveler Marco Polo. (Yes—he's a real guy; the swimming-pool game is named after HIM, see?) But Europeans had already been harvesting wheat and making wheat flour for centuries. It seems that about 12,000 years ago, after the last Ice Age ended, a certain kind of wild grass starting growing all over the place as the glaciers melted. And after about 2000 more years, people started planting it as a crop. By the time Rome became an empire, Romans ate something like 14 million bushels of wheat a year—I mean just the Romans in the city of Rome! So yes, dudes— they were into it. Majorly.

That means Europeans had flour-based foods long before 1296 when Marco Polo came back from China. (His story is AWESOME, by the way—you should check it out. Seriously.)

But wheat isn't noodles any more than an apple tree is apple sauce. It seems pasta in Europe was invented where the Arabs of North Africa and the Italians encountered each other—especially on the island of Sicily, in the Mediterranean Sea between Italy and Africa. And this happened probably by the 1100s. We don't know who did it, but by the 1400s, everybody in Italy knew about pasta, even if it was mainly rich people who ate it. After the huge plague known as the Black Death, a writer in 1370 described how the bodies of the dead were dumped into a pit, with thin layers of dirt between them—and then he compared it to lasagna, with its layers of cheese and pasta. Not too appetizing, right? But it shows how common pasta was.

And by the way, most people ate it with their fingers. Europeans didn't start using forks until about 1750, and even then a preacher declared, "God would not have given us fingers if he wanted us to use forks." Try that argument at your dinner table.

And dig this: Pasta, or "macaroni" as they called all of it at that time, had important effects on history. Dry pasta can be kept without rotting for about three years, much longer than other foods back then, so people could make long sea voyages without starving—like the one that Italian guy Columbus made to America, remember? For the same reason, dry pasta helped fight famine.

Now it's true that the Chinese did about a gazillion-and-a-half different things with noodles, like making "cat's ear noodles," "fish-flour noodles," and "across-the-bridge noodles." But when it comes to shaping pasta into different forms, the Italians are just street-rat crazy! It's estimated that Italians today eat over 60 pounds of pasta per person per year—while we Americans only eat about 20. And they have about 350 different kinds of pasta!

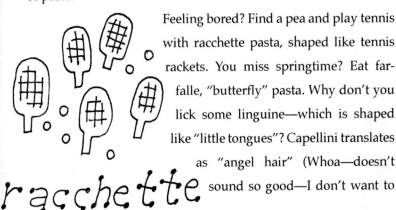

Feeling bored? Find a pea and play tennis with racchette pasta, shaped like tennis rackets. You miss springtime? Eat farfalle, "butterfly" pasta. Why don't you lick some linguine—which is shaped like "little tongues"? Capellini translates as "angel hair" (Whoa—doesn't sound so good—I don't want to swallow a halo.) Stiraletti are shaped like "little boots"—maybe your pet gerbil can wear them. There's Italian pasta shaped like pencil points, bells, rifles, shells, ears, flowers, wheels, torches, corkscrews, guitars, mushrooms, lambs' ears, stars, half moons, and worms. (Sounds like some crazy kind of Lucky Charms, huh?)

farfalle

Another kind is actually called strozzapreti, which means "strangle the priest" (maybe because he tried to keep the strozzapreti all to himself). They've even got mostaccioli—"little mustaches"—and ochi di lapo—"wolves' eyes." And if you can believe it, cavatappi, an S-shaped macaroni, is also called "Scooby Doo." I hear it's

strozzapreti

Scrappy Doo's favorite.

But before you tell me that these names are putting you off—TRY them. Come on, man—it's ITALIAN! That's a synonym for "delicious." I'd even dig into cencioni, "little tin cans"—and I'm no goat!

So maybe you're wondering why the Italians need this many different kinds of pasta. I mean, holy cannoli! I suppose it's simple: when food is good, people just want more of it. I agree! But do they really have to have spaghetti AND spaghettoni AND spaghettini? Dudes, if your waiter is a short guy named Anthony, maybe he'll bring you spaghe-teeny-Tony.

CIAO!

Okay, that's just the Dude being silly—I can't help it. The thing is, noodles are so great that noodle-nibbling has now spread around the world. Germany, for one example, is now the land of noodles and stru-dels—they got the whole kit, cat, and kaboodle!

And a Japanese man named Momofuku Ando made noodles even more popular when, in 1958, he invented instant ramen. His company still makes almost 3 billion dollars a year selling it—and it costs as little as 10 cents a package. Maybe that's why people eat ramen over 85 billion times per year—actually-factually. Japan even has a ramen museum and theme park!

TA-DA!

Like I said, noodles have changed the world. It's funny to think how something so simple can do so much good. We forget how completely we depend on food, and on the peo-ple who invented and developed better food. After all, the food we eat turns into—US! It's like Sophia Loren, this super-beautiful Italian movie star, once said about herself: "Everything you see I owe to spaghetti."

Another Italian, the famous movie director Federico Fellini, said it nicely, too: "Life," he wrote, "is a combination of magic and pasta."

But let's end with a noodle riddle—ready? Hint: Think about where it all began.

These two twins are thin.

These two twins are tall.

These two twins love noodles

but can't eat soup at all.

(The answer is at the back of the book.)

KEEP BEING AWESOME

We all know that people come in all different shapes and sizes—and that's just fine! And we all know we shouldn't worry so much about how we look. But of course it's good to be healthy. First accept your body for what it is, then make it as healthy as you can!

CHAPTER 5

My Nomination for the Snack-Bar Menu in Heaven

Alright—you're a good person, I'm a good person, our friends and families and dogs and cats and hamsters are good people, too. Even the babies in their strollers are good people, despite their tendency to howl like howler monkeys then spit up. We're all good, so we're all going to Heaven.

But what are we gonna eat up there? It's got to be abso-liciously lip-smackingly taste-errific—this is Heaven we're talking about. So I've got a nomination for the menu. The food I'm thinking of is so popular, it's probably already one of your favorites. Can you guess?

If you didn't say "pizza," I'll eat my hat. Because, Holy Water Buffalo!—pizza's awesome! (You'll understand that "water buffalo" thing in a minute.) One Saturday afternoon, my wife said, "What should we have for dinner?"

I said, "Pizza."

She said, "But we just had pizza for lunch!"

I gave her an unbelieving look. "Honey." I explained. "It's PIZZA!"

Before I tuck into a warm and wonderful pie, I always say a little blessing:

> Pizza, pizza,
> nice to meetcha!
> Hold on, Dude—
> I'm gonna eatcha!

Pizza is massively popular across the world—yet most people don't realize it's a relatively new food. The kind we eat today only became popular in the United States about fifty years ago. That means there are Americans alive now who, when they were kids, never heard of pizza! (Heartbreaking!) But now there's so much of it you can practically imagine the Statue of Liberty flinging pizzas like frisbees all over the country.

But let's start at the beginning. And that's way back, since pizza is made up of different stuff that came together over centuries. This is something cool you often see in history: good things gradually getting better.

The first thing is dough. Archaeologists think humans were making flour 10,000 years ago. Soon, people were baking dough on flat stones, especially in lands around the Mediterranean Sea. Imagine eating stuff cooked on rocks:

> THE MOM: OK, kids, dinner time! Which one do you each want?
>
> THE BROTHER: I want THIS one!
>
> THE SISTER: That's not fair! You only want it because the other rock has bugs on it!
>
> THE BROTHER: So? I called it . . .

But this was such a great and tasty idea that lots of ancient people did it. The Egyptians put oil and garlic on this flatbread—and though they'd never heard of pepperoni or Pizza Hut, they were doing their part to invent pizza! Ancient Persian soldiers supposedly baked theirs on their shields and topped it with cheese and dates—which is the best use of a shield I ever heard of.

The ancient Greeks called it "plankuntos" and added spices. (I'm glad that name didn't stick; imagine saying, "Hey, dudes—want a slice of plankuntos?") The Romans added honey, cheese, and bay leaves. The Roman poet Virgil wrote about a character who joked after a meal, "See, we devour the plates on which we feed." (Try telling your parents you want the food that lets you "devour the plates on which you feed." This may especially work if your dishwasher's broken.) And even cooler: When archaeologists dug up Pompeii, the Roman city buried by a volcano, they found shops that look just like modern pizzerias! Lucky Romans! Uh, except for that buried-by-a-volcano part.

But Holy Water Buffalo! Flatbread is a long way from pizza, even with stuff on it. (Sorry—I just love saying, "Holy Water Buffalo!" I'll explain soon.) Things got interesting again when Europeans "discovered" North and South America and Christopher Columbus himself brought back a plant called "the golden apple," which Europeans thought was curl-your-toes-and-kill-you-dead poisonous. So they used it just for decoration in gardens.

But, dudes—the "golden apple" is what we now call the tomato. And whether they make you want to gobble or gag, they're SO not poisonous! (It was called "golden," by the way, because there are yellow ones, too—calling it "the red apple" would have been a little confusing, don't you think?)

What's so great about all this, you ask? Oh, nothing much—except that we're now on the verge

of the beginning

of the very first part

of the start

of the inception of

the invention of—

modern pizza!

And for that, we go to the great Italian city of Napoli, or Naples. (I dig how the Italians say it: NOP-o-lee.)

Some brilliant Neapolitans started putting tomato sauce on their flatbread. (Yeah, they're actually called "Neapolitans." I'd vote for "Noppiloonians," but I guess it's not up to me.) And putting flatbread and tomatoes together was a big deal! The first pizzeria in the world opened in Naples in 1830. Okay, so they didn't have soda machines or those shakers of grated cheese or rock 'n' roll on the speakers—but they knew a good thing when they tasted it.

But for a LONG time, only poor people ate pizza. (Weirdly enough, it used to be the same with lobster!) Pizza was easy to make, and you ate it with your hands—which meant pizza-sellers didn't have to pay for dishes or dish-washing, which kept the prices low. This also meant that fancy rich people wouldn't lower themselves to dine on such peasant food. Which shows that pride is not only a sin—it can be its own punishment!

KEEP BEING AWESOME

People put butter and certain plant oils in lots of food, but there are much healthier choices. Olive oil is better; so are canola oil, soy oil, corn oil, and sunflower oil. And they're lip-smacking good!

Then something really cool happened, which was practically a fairy tale—only it had pizza in it, which most fairy tales don't. In 1889, Italy's Queen Margherita, wife of King Umberto, got curious about this new food, so one night she called a pizza-maker named Raffaele Esposito and asked him to bring pizza to the palace. He made three kinds, but her favorite had the same colors as the Italian flag: red tomato sauce, white mozzarella cheese, and green basil leaves. She loved it—I mean, she totally grooved on it! (That mozzarella-and-basil kind is called "pizza margherita" to this day!) And since the people thought she was hecka great, pizza got super-popular.

And check it out: Raffaele made the first pizza delivery! (I wonder if the Queen gave him a tip . . .)

And here's where the water buffaloes come in. (See? I didn't forget.) When European Crusaders came back from the Middle East, some actually brought Asian water buffaloes with them. Water-buffalo milk is what you make traditional mozzarella cheese from—the numero-uno pizza cheese! So pizza even has some of Asia in it!

(I don't know about you, but when I think of Italy, I don't picture water buffaloes. What's next—giraffes in Sweden? Hmm . . . I wonder what kind of cheese you'd get from giraffe milk . . .)

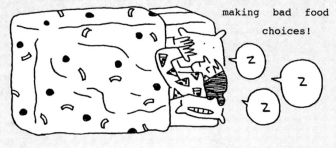

KEEP BEING AWESOME

Believe it or not, your sleep has something to do with all this, too. Because young people need lots of sleep, and many don't get enough. And that can lead to problems like being over-weight, not to mention feeling bad and making bad food choices!

Still, we're not quite up to the pizza Americans know and love. But history was on the march, and the wheels of progress were rolling and all that. People from everywhere started coming to the U.S., and a lot of them were Italians, especially around 1900.

So, naturally, they brought their recipes. Would you leave that one behind? I mean, come on—it's PIZZA!

The first American pizza came from a grocery store in New York City in 1897. Gennaro Lombardi owned the store, and his worker Antonio Totonno started making pizza. I think somebody should write a poem about him. Like,

> Antonio,
> you're the only-o
> true super-hero
> and that's no baloney-o.
> You made pizza
> for us to eat-sa,
> even if you didn't have
> delivery by phone-io.

delizioso

Okay, maybe not that poem. Still, you gotta be grateful to Gennaro and Antonio! Their store is still open today. (But don't buy the pizza in the front window—I hear it's been there since 1897.)

(And maybe it's GOOD that modern pizza wasn't invented in America. If it had to be red, white, and blue, that'd be, what? Tomatoes, mozzarella—and blueberries? Eww.)

Even then, though, most Americans had never heard of pizza. But along came World War II. American soldiers fighting in Italy came back raving about this delizioso Italian dish. Soon it was the cool new thing. And it just took off from there. By the 1970s, Americans were eating two billion pizzas a year. Today, its popularity is still spreading—all over the world! For example, some people in South Africa made one of the biggest pizzas ever, which was over 122 feet across. (Yikes! The pepperonis must have been like manhole covers!)

And now, Americans eat 350 slices PER SECOND—which adds up to 100 acres of pizza a day! (I'd like to farm THAT hundred acres.)

And people have invented all different kinds. This awesome dude from Chicago named Ike Sewell invented deep-dish pizza (which is Rude Dude's favorite). Then people came up with pizza dough mix, pizza chain restaurants, pizza delivery (with that little plastic table-thing that keeps the pizza from sticking to the top of the box), and different forms like calzones and stuffed-crust and dessert pizza, and even pizza on a stick.

And people started putting all kinds of stuff on their pies, like octopus and cherries and corn and tofu and oysters and dandelions—I'm for real about this. People have even tried peanut butter and jelly, bacon and eggs, and mashed potatoes. Mexicans often put ketchup on pizza; their delivery-pizza comes with ketchup packets. In China, they use fresh bamboo. In Maine, boiled clams. In Japan, eels or—I'm not making this up—black squid ink! The French often garnish pizza with snails. (At least if those little dudes try to escape, you can catch them.) My point here is that, somewhere on Planet Earth right now, someone's probably putting a kitchen sink on their pizza and licking their lips. (You know that old saying, right? "Everything but the kitchen sink . . . "?)

Of course, you've gotta draw the line somewhere. I have a rule of thumb: Don't put anything on a pizza unless it's actually food. Don't let your three-year-old sister, for example, sprinkle it with glitter. Glue's not too good either, even if some silly little kids eat it sometimes. And of course, no coins or screws or mousetraps or that kind of stuff. (You probably knew that already—but I'm all about safety.)

Now there may be an exception here. Say Butch, your cousin twelve-times removed, is in prison and you want to get him out. You might put one of those big metal files in a pizza and send it to him, so he can saw through the bars. This, of course, would have to be thick-crust pizza, or, you know, the guards would see the file.

But actually, since it's pizza, I bet the guards would sneak a slice or two themselves, and find the file. Sorry, Cousin Butch!

But your trick might work anyway, since they'd probably say, "Heck, let the prisoner have the file—we'll keep the pie!"

Like I keep saying—it's PIZZA!

A Poem for Dessert

PIZZA BOX BLUES

Well, the sun comes up this morning
and I hang my head so low.
Just can't shake these dreary blues,
can't let the sweet dream go:
'Cuz I look out on the table—
and my soul falls to my socks:
ain't nothing on it
but a sad ole'
grease-stained
empty
pizza box.

Well, we lived it up last evening,
pizza-partying till dawn.
Seemed there'd never be an end
to sprinkling Parmesan.
Now I look out on the table—
my heart heavier than rocks:
ain't nothing on it
but a sad ole'
grease-stained
empty
pizza box.

So listen, pizza eaters—
it can't go on and on!
The thing is, once you eat it,
your pizza will be gone.
You'll look out on the table
(till that d'livery guy next knocks):
won't be nothing on it
but a sad ole'
grease-stained
oh-so-empty
pizza box.

CHAPTER 6

LET'S WOK AND ROLL

So picture this: It's Christmas Eve at the Dude's house. One of the greatest nights of the year. The family's together, it's the season of joy and cheer, we want music and meaning and fun and . . .

Well, come on, dudes—you know! FOOD!

Human celebrations have almost always included food. My family loves to celebrate for any reason—especially Christmas. So what food do you think we have on Christmas Eve?

Would you believe . . . egg rolls?

It's true! Our ancestors came from Ireland, Scotland, Germany, and France. So we eat cookies and puff pastries and "pigs-in-a-blanket" and other Euro-American stuff like that. (It's weird, isn't it? "Pigs-in-a-blanket" are actually hot dogs. But "hot dogs" are actually—you guessed it—pig. Well, mostly.) But on this most wonderful of nights, we also just totally nosh on that little delicacy from Asia. Because once Chinese food really hit America, we all started to "wok and roll."

Of course, that's a very American way of doing things when you think about it. The U.S.A. is the invented country, the country made up of people from all over the place! Even Native Americans, the first Americans, originally crossed the Bering Strait

into North America. Geeze, I never thought about that—they came from Asia— maybe THAT'S why it's so American to love egg rolls!

Because, dudes—we DO! I can't even begin to guess how many egg rolls Americans eat per year, but I'll tell you what—it's a lip-smackin' lot!

The name of this chapter might have tipped you off to what we're going to talk about. A "wok" is a deep pan or skillet for quick-cooking food, invented in China—and it's responsible for some ding-dong delicious stuff. And with all the Asian food now in the U.S., it's only natural that we'd consider it as American as rock 'n' roll. "Wok and roll" is an old joke—well, actually, not that old. Because America, always attracting immigrants, didn't start seeing big numbers of Asian immigrants until

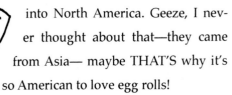

the middle of the 1800s. In my opinion, we should have started earlier! Because Asians have contributed so much to what it means to be American. And at the moment, the Dude is hungry—and when he's hungry, he thinks about food—and all the Asian food in America today makes the Dude very, very happy. And egg rolls are at the top of the list!

But before we talk about egg rolls, we've got to talk about something else: China.

Don't know if you know it, dudes, but China is a major, majorly awesome country. I don't always agree with what today's Chinese government does, but I've got to admit, when it comes to world history, China is—well, IMPORTANT. It's been around for a long, long time, and the Chinese have invented or developed all kinds of great stuff (which they continue to do). And there are currently more than one BILLION Chinese people out of seven billion humans on Earth; there are more Chinese than any other kind of people. So if some E.T. from outer space wanted to see "Earthlings," the best bet would be to introduce him or her—or it—to some Chinese people. (If any space aliens are reading this—sorry about that "it.")

Americans don't always get this. And part of the problem is pure culture. I mean, come on—people get used to what they get used to, know what I mean? Americans don't always understand Chinese culture, and Chinese don't always understand American culture. Especially when it comes to food.

There's a saying among food historians: Human beings eat anything that won't kill them—and even some things that WILL! For example, some Japanese are into an expensive form of puffer fish that actually has enough poison in it to sometimes kill the person who eats it! And every year people die in Europe and North America from poisonous mushrooms.

This leads to my second point: "weird" food.

Let's get real. It's obvious that what people in one culture eat isn't always considered edible by people from another culture. And food is a very important part of Chinese culture; one of the most common greetings in Chinese is "Have you eaten?" So let's talk about some things the Chinese eat, or have eaten (because some of these things aren't eaten in China any more).

But before we start, we need to get one thing straight. You think American food is "normal"? Oh no, my dear dudes—it all depends. There's plenty of stuff Americans love that seems bizarre to other cultures, or has only recently been accepted by them. The Chinese have a saying: "Some prefer carrots while others like cabbage." Okay, not exactly a zinger like "What goes around comes around"—but a good point. There's a similar saying in English: "One man's meat is another man's poison."

(By the way, the Chinese have another saying, too: "a hat-wearing monkey"—which means, you may seem to be the real deal, but you're a big faker. I love that! Just thought I'd mention it.)

For one example, consider cheese. I've talked about it before. Imagine what it sounds like to people who aren't used to it! Some Chinese thought of it—and some still do—as "the putrefied mucous discharge of an animal's guts." Translation: Rotten snot from critter guts. OK. As a cheese-MANI-AC, I don't agree. But I see what they mean. In fact, many Chinese are "lactose-intolerant" as adults, meaning their bodies just can't handle dairy foods like milk or cheese.

And what about eating cows? Burger-crazy America thinks that's as natural as apple pie. (Ever consider how weird "apple pie" is to people who live in the tropics, where apples don't grow?) In Japan, deeply influenced by Buddhist ideas about not killing animals, people didn't eat beef for centuries (although eating fish was, apparently, OK). And although some Japanese tasted beef when Europeans first showed up, most didn't. I've read that the first killing of a cow for food in Japan happened in 1853, after the American naval commander Matthew Perry had arrived with a fleet to "open" Japan to the West.

And think about peanut butter. The Dude thinks peanut butter is a divine gift—I have to keep myself from eating it by the spoonful. But at one point in China, many people considered peanuts only fit for animals. (Excuse me—the Dude must be an animal—because just the mention of peanut butter made me hungry. So I'm off to get a spoonful.

Ah—there. Now I can go on.)

But let me throw in one more thing: Before you judge the Chinese as "gross" for eating things you vmay not want to—keep in mind that you may never in your life have felt as hungry as lots of people did in the past (and as some still do today). China has had many terrible famines, times when there was so little food that people actually starved to death.

In fact, Americans may turn up their noses at certain Chinese foods because the Chinese are more open to different foods than we are. There's a saying in China, usually directed toward people who live in Guangdong Province: "They'll eat anything with legs besides a table, and anything with wings besides an airplane." (Guangdong, by the way, is also known as "Kwang-Tung," and its capital city is called "Canton" in English.)

So—keeping in mind that Europeans such as the French eat horses and snails—and that both Africans and Southeast Asians eat fried caterpillars—and that Japanese sometimes order squid ink on their pizza (remember that mouth-watering, well, "mouth-inking" fact?)—and that some

Americans eat tripe, which is cow guts—let's look at some strange Chinese foods.

In the past, Chinese emperors used to command banquets with at least 100 different dishes. That's a lot! I don't mean that only the Chinese ate a lot of different things; if you go back far enough, all human beings ate basically whatever they could get. But it's true: Chinese people have eaten things like "flattened dog meat" (Yikes! Did they have cars back then?)—a soup of camel's hooves that cost 1000 ounces of gold—chicken feet—goose-foot-webs (you know, the part that helps them swim better, like scuba fins)—barbecued elephant trunks (Good grief! How'd they GET them?!)—python—rotten fish—bear paws—ape lips—even "honeyed...deer brains," leopard fetus, puppies, and pig-stomach soup. (But take note: not ALL Chinese people ate all this stuff; some Chinese, for example, made fun of people from Fukien and Chekiang for eating frogs.)

And even today, some Chinese sometimes eat things like jellyfish, owl soup, dried sea horses, and deep-fried pigeon. (Pigeon! That'd sure be handy if you lived in a big city!) Ask yourself: Why should we think of eating pigeon as any weirder than eating chicken? We're just used to chicken! In Guangdong, one form of cough medicine includes fried duck gizzards (that's an organ birds have—I know some Americans who also eat them!) And don't forget the amazingly-named dish "Dragon, Phoenix, and Tiger"—which is actually snake, chicken, and cat.

KEEP BEING AWESOME

We all get thirsty, of course. But some of the worst things for us are drinks such as sugary soda. The good news is that water is WONDERFUL! And hey—it comes right out of the faucet! If you drink milk, drink fat-free. Oh, and be careful about drinking fruit juice—EATING fruit is awesome, but fruit juice isn't very good for you.

One writer talks about a special banquet in Beijing: The main course was the famous Peking Duck—but in separate dishes, the diners got ducks' kidneys, livers, intestines, brains, and deep-fried ducks' tongues. (I didn't even know ducks had tongues—I guess the quacking's gotta come from somewhere.) Speaking of ducks, a popular food in China is "hundred-year-old" or "thousand-year-old" duck eggs—which are actually about two to four months old. Other favorites are shark-fin soup, bird's-nest soup, dried balloon-fish heads, and sea cucumbers (animals that are pretty much what their name suggests, except rubbery and kinda squishy). Consider also these current dishes: "Caterpillar Fungus Duck," "Flower Mushroom Frog," and "Crab and Fish Stomachs."

But, again, just think about all this for a minute. "Ethnocentrism" means thinking your own culture's better than all the others—which really doesn't make sense! If you grew up eating dog or snake or whatever, it'd taste just fine to you. After all, most Americans don't have any trouble eating pigs. (I wonder what pigs might say about that. Maybe they'd be all, "Dudes! Don't eat us! Eat snails and horses!")

There's a great story about how anybody can be ignorant and silly about new or different foods. Centuries ago, many Chinese, especially in the north, had never seen bananas because they can't grow there. One day, a great northern warlord was at a feast in Beijing, and at the end, the servants brought out a huge bowl of fruit. The warlord took a banana and ate it—peel and all! The host, not wanting to embarrass him, didn't say anything but simply picked up another banana and peeled it, to show how it was done. But the warlord was too embarrassed to admit his mistake. "I like these," he lied, "but I prefer them with the peel on." So he ate another, including the peel, to show he always did it that way.

Okay, compadres—I know what you may be feeling at this point. Like, "Rude Dude, all these weird foods—gag me with a spoon! It's too much!" But my point is not to gross you out. It's just to remind you that people eat lots of different stuff. And that we often assume that only our own food is any good. So when one kind of food jumps from one culture to other cultures—well, that's something special.

And that's exactly what egg rolls did.

For the last thousand years, the Chinese have also been eating spring rolls (more or less the same as egg rolls, though lighter and with thinner crusts). "Egg" rolls traditionally had dough made with egg. The basic deal is a pastry wrapped around delicious shredded stuff. And you can put lots of different things inside—meat, fish, vegetables, etc.—there are hundreds and hundreds of recipes! (I just pray somebody out there is stuffing them with peanut butter cups).

These rolls were popular during Chinese New Year, also called the "Spring Festival"—so they got the name "spring rolls." And because they had a nice golden color, they symbolized a gold nugget, which symbolized being rich—so people liked having them at banquets. (Can you imagine, for example, lettuce made to look like dollar bills or tater tots shaped like  diamonds?) Egg rolls can be found in countries all over Asia, including the Phillipines, where they make a delicious larger version called  "lumpia."

So how did egg rolls get to the land of the good old Red, White, and Blue?

The very first Americans to eat Chinese food did so in China—they came on a ship, *The Empress of China*, back in 1784. But it took a while for Chinese food to come to America. That began when so many Chinese traveled to California (or "Gold Mountain," as the Chinese called it) for the Gold Rush in 1849—you know, like the 49ers. (Just to compare, other kinds of delicious Asian food—like Japanese, Thai, and Vietnamese—were almost unknown in America till the 1970s!)

As time passed, a lot of this Chinese food was changed to fit American tastes, and some supposedly Chinese food was even invented here—like chow mien, sweet and sour pork, General Tso's Chicken, or the famous "pu pu platter." (OK, I know you're gonna laugh—go ahead and get it over with.)

In the 1800s, a lot more Chinese came to America—and soon there was a Chinese restaurant in every major American city or town. But the food wasn't all that popular till the 1920s, when cool Roaring 20s–type people started eating it because it was so different. It wasn't till after World War II, though, that it really made it big across the U.S. The first time "spring roll" appeared in print in English was in 1943.

Historians think egg rolls probably made it to America with all the other Chinese food that came in the 1880s—and then also changed to meet American tastes. (Chinese egg rolls, for example, are usually shaped like small flutes.) We know for sure, though, that, from then on, they just got more and more popular. As one writer says, "Egg rolls are now an unremarkable part of the American landscape." However, I've got to add a couple things here: First, he should have said "a remarkable part"—and second, you don't exactly see them sprouting up from fields and farms. But of course I know what he meant.

I suppose if somebody built a huge temple with spires and floodlights and a ginormous towering statue of an egg roll right in the middle—well, the Dude is one American who'd get on his knees and worship that sucker! Egg rolls are now pretty much as American as—well, as pizza, hamburgers, chocolate, and the rest.

And so, my fellow wok-and-rollers—consider the glorious story of the egg roll, that Emperor of Appetizers, and think about how human beings all over the world are getting more and more connected, and having more and more influence on each other, in big ways and little ways. I mean, this is just a very human thing to do.

So dudes, when it comes to different cultures—do the truly human thing and be open minded! Don't be a hat-wearing monkey!

And if you happen to be throwing a party or something, and you plan on serving egg rolls—do me a favor, will you? Drop the Dude a line.

You invite me—I'm there!

A Poem for Dessert

THE TRICK TO EATING EELS

The trick to eating eels
is not to feel one—

(not rubber-toy-type eels—
I mean a real one).

Feels kinda like a grape,
a freshly peeled one

or like a lump of ooze,
a just-congealed one.

I don't think it's wise
for you to steal one,

especially if you plan
to make a meal, son.

'Cuz I don't think you'll feel
that you've had real fun

once your Eel Supreme
Full-Meal Deal's done.

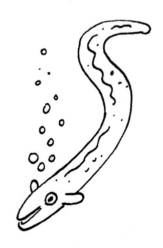

CHAPTER 7

ONE SMART COOKIE

OK, dudes, let's get all Einstein for a minute. Think about stuff that tells the future.

Of course, nothing can exactly predict what will happen—but people like to pretend. So, a crystal ball, right? Or the silly and lovable "Magic 8-Ball." People have tried all kinds of things; ancient cultures actually cut open birds or sheep and saw the future in marks on their innards. (Seems like the only thing THAT would predict is that you're having bird or sheep for lunch.)

But what about a food that predicts?

I can only think of one. Come on—it's almondy or vanilla-tasting—and you get it after dinner—but only at a certain kind of restaurant . . .

OH NO

Here's the biggest hint: if you just pop it in your mouth—you'll never know what the future holds!

That's right: the fortune cookie. It's amazing how much we love them. There are almost three billion fortune cookies made every year. (With that many fortunes flying around, it's a wonder anything ever surprises us!) I can't think of any other food that gives people messages. Oh, sure, a cake with "HAPPY BIRTHDAY, GODZILLA!" or something written on it. But you've got to admit—fortune cookies have a LOT to say! Compared to them, other food is pretty mute.

And their history is surprising. Plus, it shows how different cultures are always copying and trading and inventing, and how the world at any given moment is a big mixed-up ball of copying and trading and inventing—and how lots of really great things come from that.

KEEP BEING AWESOME

People need a little sodium to stay healthy. But most of us get way too much salt in our diets! A lot of it comes in food we buy already prepared. Some companies are putting less salt in their food products, but not all. Eating more fruits and vegetables, eating more fresh food, and just eating less junk food (like chips and soda) are all ways to take in less salt.

Maybe you're thinking, "Dude—what's the big mystery? Fortune cookies are from China." But I wouldn't bet your eggroll on that. (And you KNOW I'd love to eat your eggroll.) This story has more twists than—well, than there are folds in a fortune cookie.

Check it out: In 1844, a guy from New Jersey named James Marshall, farming in Missouri, got malaria—which as you know, dudes, is NOT good. His doctor said a better climate would help him, so he took a wagon train to Oregon, then California. And while working on a sawmill in 1848, he was checking over the ditch that drained from the waterwheel and noticed something shiny. It was gold.

Now some people really get ants in their pants when it comes to gold. This discovery brought people from all over the world to California; we call it the Gold Rush. Plenty of Chinese, too, many of them dirt poor, came to "Gum Sann" or Gold Mountain, as they called America. (Remember, I told you about that before?)

It's very sad to say that lots of people in America back then—whose own ancestors, after all, had come from other countries—treated the Chinese terribly. The United States passed laws banning more Chinese people from entering America. These "Chinese Exclusion Acts" were just plain racist—and, if you ask me, wicked mean. But despite all they had to endure, the Chinese in America kept on working hard and helping to build the country.

Of course they brought their own recipes with them. And although their first restaurants were for other Chinese, over time non-Chinese Americans started eating Chinese food, too. Today there are more Chinese restaurants in America than there are McDonald's, Wendy's, and Burger Kings combined. Dang!

But what I'm talking about here is only the spread of Chinese food in general. Because back then, nobody in any of those many, many restaurants was making or eating fortune cookies. Why? Simple: fortune cookies are not Chinese. Even so, this was important because Americans had to get used to Chinese food before the fortune cookie could become popular.

I grew up in Colorado, back when the only foreign restaurants we had were Mexican and Chinese—and I never ate Chinese till I was an adult. I actually didn't like it! Which is Weird City to the max, because, if you knew me, you'd know I'm now coo-coo-for-Cocoa-Puffs over Chinese food. Obviously, both me and the rest of America have "gotten used to" Chinese food (at least the American version of it—but that's another story).

But here, oh my young dudes, we see something very basic about human beings. The thing is, whatever culture you grew up in, you usually take that way of life for granted; the stuff that's around you all the time, you just assume it's normal. But that's not necessarily true, since most cultures have certain parts to them— like ways of doing things, or certain ideas, or types of food—that other cultures don't. And what seems weird to one culture can seem perfectly normal to another (which I also told you about before).

Americans take fortune cookies for granted—but the Chinese in China don't even know about them! So a fortune cookie is "weird"—at least to the Chinese.

Of course, it's really no weirder than, say, our old friend the Magic 8-Ball. Try explaining that one to somebody from a different culture: "See, in America, we have a game called pool, and it has a black ball with an 8 on it. So we make a plastic version of that ball, only bigger—then we fill it with water—then we put this little pyramid of plastic in it, with stuff written on the sides 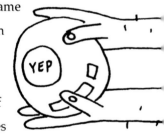 like 'My sources say no' and 'Signs point to yes.' Then, if we want to know what's going to happen, we shake the Magic 8-Ball and read which saying comes up to the little window in the bottom. That's how we get answers to all our questions in life."

What—THAT'S not weird?!

But back to fortune cookies. Jennifer 8. Lee is an expert on them.

(I KNOW!—not only is her middle name a number, which is cool enough, but she's a fortune-cookie expert! Awesome!) When she recently gave fortune cookies to people in China, they were surprised to find pieces of paper in their mouths. She also learned that a Chinese woman manufacturing fortune cookies there has to put instructions on the wrappers so people know to get the fortunes out first. The Chinese reaction is, "Americans are so strange! Why are they putting pieces of paper in their cookies?"

KEEP BEING AWESOME
Another cool thing is that, according to the experts, making small changes in your diet can make you much healthier over time. So you don't have to go whole hog—you can just keep working on it in small ways. Yo!

The Chinese don't even have a single name for fortune cookies. They've been called "good luck cookies," "good luck sweet cookies," "good luck dry cookies," "happiness dry cookies," "label-words cookies," "lucky label-words cookies," "good luck label-words cookies," and even "divining cookies" (that means "predicting the future"). I don't know about you, but "label-words cookie" doesn't exactly make me hungry—and I'm known in my family as the Cookie Monster.

Can you imagine a similar situation with, say, hamburgers in the U.S.? Imagine people calling them "flat-meat sandwiches" or "tasty flat-meat sandwiches" or "happy grilled flat-meat sandwiches" or "grilled bunned beef-shreds" or "this-cow-will-moo-no-more sandwiches"?

And you actually believed that fortune cookies came from China, didn't you?! Bet you feel silly now, huh? Don't. Because everybody seems to believe it. And it makes sense, because unless you buy yours from a fortune cookie factory (yes, there's really such a thing), you usually only get them after dinner at Chinese restaurants.

So now your hot-buzzing little minds are screaming, "Dude! If they're not Chinese—what are they?!"

Let me tell you what happened—it's so cool!

Now please understand: You'll hear people tell all kinds of stories about the origin of fortune cookies. They're like hamburgers that way—so famous that lots of people want to take credit. But thanks to Yasuko Nakamachi, we know the truth.

And here's where we have to talk about something called "primary source evidence."

Sounds kind of funky, doesn't it? But it's actually very important. Say you and your brother or sister or dog or cat or parakeet got in a fight. (OK, first of all, you shouldn't fight—especially not with dogs, cats, or parakeets.) You were asking the Magic 8-Ball if you're gonna be president, and your brother or sister said, "Stop hogging it!" And you said, "You can have it in five minutes." But when five minutes came, you didn't want to give it up (mainly because it kept saying things like "Reply hazy—try again" and "Better not tell you now"). So your brother or sister went ballistic and told your mom or dad or grandma or babysitter or dog or cat or parakeet (oh—sorry—I didn't mean those last three). And although part of you knew it wasn't exactly true, you said, "I never said that!" Who would your mom or dad or grandma or babysitter believe?

Well, what if your brother or sister used a hidden microphone to record you saying, "You can have it at 3:35"—what then? That's right—you're toast. That's primary source evidence. Historians love it, because it can tell them what really happened. It's called "primary" because it comes from the very time in history the historian is studying. If somebody said, "The Pilgrims ate turkey at the first Thanksgiving" and we somehow got an actual video of them tearing into rubber chickens—well, that would be extremely silly, but it would also be proof they didn't eat turkey!

And Yasuko Nakamachi isn't just anybody. For one thing, she's a researcher and scholar at Kanagawa University. And she spent six whole years—and traveled all over the place—trying to figure this out.

Her first piece of evidence was finding restaurants in Kyoto, Japan, that make what they call *tsujiura senbei*—"fortune crackers." One of these bakeries opened in 1934. But then she found

something even better: a drawing from an old book that shows a Japanese man making these same fortune crackers. The book is from 1878—a good bit earlier than all the claims by Japanese and Chinese immigrants in California that they invented fortune cookies. There's even mention of the crackers in a book written before 1843! The Japanese "fortune crackers" aren't exactly the same—they're bigger and darker, sweet but also flavored with ginger and miso (a common Japanese soup). But get this: They had fortunes tucked into them—not inside, but squeezed into the fold.

Can you believe it? Fortune cookies are actually . . . Japanese! When I heard that, I was so surprised you could've knocked me over with a feather.

But if they're Japanese, you ask, why are they only served in Chinese restaurants?

Ah, history is such a trip!

It seems that Makoto Hagiwara, a Japanese-American man who owned the Japanese Tea Garden in San Francisco, was the first person to serve the American version of the fortune cookie.

In any case, some Chinese-Americans began making them, too. Like I said, good ideas tend to spread.

This is where the story gets sad again. Remember how so many Americans were mean and unfair to Chinese people who came here? Well, it happened to Japanese people as well. And the worst was during World War II.

After Japan launched a surprise attack on Pearl Harbor, Americans were—understandably—angry and fearful. We declared war on Japan. But we also made a huge mistake. Because there were lots of Japanese-AMERICANS living on the West Coast, people who were born here, who were helping to make America what it is. (For example, a lot of Japanese-American men joined the Army and fought in Europe—and their units won more medals than any others!) But huge numbers of Japanese-Americans were put into "internment camps" in far-off places during the war, as if they were enemies. That included Mr. Hagiwara and his family. Now, I ask you: is that any way to treat the guy who brought the fortune cookie to America?!

With so many Japanese bakeries closed, Chinese-Americans saw an opening and began making and selling even more fortune cookies. And when American soldiers came home from the Pacific through California, they learned about fortune cookies and started spreading the word across America. (Check it out: The biggest fortune cookie maker in the U.S. today is in Brooklyn, New York!) It got to the point where everyone believed fortune cookies were as Chinese as Peking duck.

How good is all this evidence? Strong enough to convince even Jenny Lee. And the fact that Jenny Lee writes for *The New York Times*, the most famous newspaper in America, doesn't hurt either— because *The New York Times* has a great reputation for accuracy.

And even more: Jenny Lee is Chinese-American. So you could forgive her for wanting such a great food to come from China. When she found out it didn't, as she says, it "was like learning there was no Santa Claus and I was adopted at the same time." But you just can't argue with good primary source evidence. And don't worry, kids. There is a Santa Claus.

Check it out: because of all this great evidence, I had a really fun moment the other day.

I was at a Chinese restaurant in San Francisco's Chinatown. When the waiter brought fortune cookies, I said to my family, "Anybody want a Japanese cookie?"

The waiter, somewhat rudely, corrected me. "Not Japanese—CHINESE."

But he was wrong—and I was right!

I so rule.

Whatever people may believe, though, fortune cookies are really, really popular. You love them, I love them, and so do the babies in their strollers. So let's try to predict the future ourselves: do you think people will keep eating them?

I'd say all signs point to yes.

A Poem for Dessert

WHEN CAMELS CAME TO TEA

Camels caused confusion
when we sat down for tea—
I had to wonder at the camel
sitting next to me.

He wore a lovely jacket,
which I could not see through,
and so I felt perplexed:
Would it be one hump, or two?

CHAPTER 8

"WHOA—THAT IS SO CHICKEN 65!"

Yes, my young dudes and dudettes, I know this is a spacy-sounding title for a chapter. Let me explain.

My family and I sometimes go to this great Indian restaurant called "Sneha." (That's Hindi for "love" or "sweetheart." The owner named the restaurant for his little daughter— which is cool!)

At Sneha, they serve a chicken dish in this hot red sauce which is just freaky ultralicious. I feel like steam-whistles shoot out of my ears, my eyeballs pop out, and fireworks go off around my head. It's not that it's super-hot— just incredibly, brain-smackingly good. It's called "Chicken 65."

Why's it called that? We actually don't know. We know it came from South India, some say from the city of Hyderabad, some Chennai. (Sounds a lot like the fight over who invented burgers, huh?) At first I thought it might be made from 65-year-old chickens—but "cluckily" that's not the case. Some say it's because they used 65-day-old chickens. But holy poultry—would you refuse to eat a 66-day-old chicken? Other people say it's because the dish was invented in 1965, or that they used 65 kinds of chilies to make it. Dudes—your guess is as good as mine!

YUM!

Anyway, being the cool cat and down dog that I am, I started calling anything I really like "Chicken 65." It's not for stuff that's just OK—it has to be INTENSELY, EXTRA-DUDICALLY perfecto.

As in, "Let's go to Disneyland—that would be Chicken 65!" Or "Have you heard that new song by Lady Googoo—it's SO Chicken 65!"

KEEP BEING AWESOME

If I said, "Open your mouth and close your eyes," you'd be suspicious, right? After all, you don't want to put just ANYTHING in there! One way to stay healthy is to read food labels so you know exactly what you're getting. Open your mouth—but keep your eyes open too!

Hmm

(And since I, the Dude, am mad with power and love to mess with the world, I humbly request that you, my dear readers, start using this phrase in your daily life. As in, "I finished my homework—I feel so Chicken 65!" Or "Hey, man, your new hoodie is Chicken 65!" Or even texting: "movie 2NTE? will be chikn 65.")

So why am I telling you all this? Partly because this is a book about food, so a food expression only makes sense. But also because, in this final chapter, I wanted to emphasize how cool I think food history is, and I needed a way to say that. I mean, come on! Who would have thought Italians got water buffaloes from Asia to make pizza cheese? Who would have imagined hamburgers had anything to do with Mongols? Who could have known cacao beans used to be money? Who could have even dreamed that ancient Chinese big-shots ate ape lips?!

I also love how food history shows the ways different cultures make connections with each other, like I keep saying. Remember way back in Chapter 1, when I told you that Kit Kat bars are from England? There's plenty more like that. Oranges aren't originally from Florida, but China. Japanese kids on vacation in Hawaii or Paris will line up at McDonald's to eat "Biggu Makku"—because they're homesick. Writing this book reminded me that, as my wife keeps saying, "We're all more alike than we are different."

My daughter once went to a party at her Vietnamese friend Lindsey's house. The egg rolls, my daughter said, were delicious. So she asked if they'd used some traditional Vietnamese recipe. No, her friend told her; they bought 'em at Costco.

In a way, this book is only partly about food. It's also about the fascinating nature of history itself—the endless, endlessly-amazing story of human beings and all the things they think, feel, and do. I mean, how much more Chicken 65 can it get?

But I also have to tell you a few other things before I'm done.

Okay, so the Dude was once young like you, and he used to watch cartoons, and there was one called *The Jetsons*, and it was about the future. The Jetson family had a flying car and a robot-maid and lots of stuff that came down conveyor belts (for some reason, conveyor belts seemed real future-y back then). And I seem to remember that nobody in the future ate food— you just swallowed a pill every morning, and that gave you everything you needed.

Doesn't sound all that great, huh? But don't worry! I can tell you with confidence: Not. Gonna. Happen.

I'll give you one reason: Even when I was a little shaver (well, I actually didn't have anything to shave back then)—even when I was a little kid, I couldn't help wondering what those pills would taste like.

See my point? People LOVE to eat. We can't help it; we're made that way. So even if somebody invented such a pill—which is pretty unlikely—who would want to give up stuff like pizza and chocolate and the rest and just suck down pills? Way not cool.

On the other hand, the food we eat, the way we grow it or get it, the way we prepare it, the way we buy and sell it—some of that is definitely going to change. And it should.

But don't worry—it won't freak everybody out or anything. The government, for example, isn't going to force you to eat banana slugs. As things change, we'll change with them. Humans are always changing how we live in one way or another, and food is no exception—you know that from reading this book! There are some important changes being made today because people have been thinking about how we can improve the world of food.

A lot of smart, expert-type people are saying we should eat healthier. That's important—of course. For example, one very Chicken 65 thing about being healthier is . . . you feel better! And you do the stuff you do a lot better, too, which also makes you happier.

Plus, we also have to change some of our eating habits so we can take better care of the environment. If we ate fewer burgers, for example, there'd be fewer rain forests cut down to make grazing land for cattle, and—believe it or not—less gas from cows warming up the atmosphere. (Isn't that crazy? Cow pooting actually affects the planet!) It's also important that the people who produce our food, wherever they live, get treated fairly—for example, the people who grow coffee. They deserve decent working conditions and fair prices for their crops.

Another thing we can all do is be smarter about food advertising.

Look—I love toys too, like the cool flying Superman figure I got from a burger place. But you shouldn't let toys or stickers or stuff like that make you decide what you're going to eat (or what you're going to bug your parents to buy). Same for cereal boxes with cool stuff on the outside. There are LOTS of kids in America, and when you put together all the money they spend on food, it adds up to BILLIONS OF DOLLARS. Kids, for example, were McDonald's most loyal customers, even when the McDonald brothers built their first restaurant. Advertisers know this, so they try to get you

KEEP BEING AWESOME

When the Dude says "Keep being awesome," he means it. One of the most important parts of eating healthy is simply BELIEVING that you should take good care of yourself—because you deserve it. If you really believe that, you'll try harder. And you SHOULD believe it. After all, it's true. And the Dude thinks so too!

I KNOW IT!

to buy THEIR stuff. (Sheesh—McDonald's even builds PLAYGROUNDS to get you to eat there!) I'm not saying they're all cheating you, but don't be like a fish who bites at anything that looks like a worm—because it might be a hook. Know what I mean?

And since you're a kid and your body and mind are growing and the whole nine yards, it's obvious you gotta look after yourself— you know it, I know it, and the babies in their strollers know it. My deal is that I love the foods I love, and I eat them— but the ones that aren't that good for me, I don't eat very often. Which only makes it more fun when I do. And I try to eat a lot of different healthy stuff on a regular basis.

Let me give you some examples.

My very smart (and very cute) wife just read this article about movie popcorn—you know, the DELICIOUS kind that grabs your nose by the collar and says "EAT ME, EAT ME!" (Well, no, of course my nose doesn't have a collar—but you know what I mean.) But guess what: They usually pop that popcorn in coconut oil. Now I've got nothing against something as cool as a coconut (food, drink, clothing, shelter, and weapon all in one). But coconut-oil popcorn isn't good for you! Most movie popcorn is like DRENCHED in fat. My wife can't take much fat—she's got a kind of "butterometer" in her body. Too much butter gives her a stomachache. And most movie popcorn just kills her! (Which is a sign to me, since her butterometer is telling us all something.)

My solution? I won't totally give it up—but I'm only going to eat it once a year or so. Some people stay away from it completely.

You gotta eat in moderation. So what does "moderation" mean? Well—you can't have cheeseburgers for breakfast, pizza topped with chocolate chip cookies for lunch, ice cream and potato chips for dinner, and then pop some peanut butter cups every time you have a headache. No, dudes—don't even think about it.

Instead, follow the US Department of Agriculture's MyPlate diagram and get plenty of exercise. The good news here is that the best way to exercise is to play—I mean the kind of playing where you move your body. Having strong thumbs ain't exactly a sign of health, if you know what I mean. I, for example, love riding my bike, and I do it all the time.

And I hope, oh dear boy-dudes and girl-dudes, that you're not guilty of that horrible sin I call "Veg Prej." Catch my drift? Vegetables are seriously, stupendously good for us. So don't be PREJudiced against VEGetables! (Maybe we should call it "preg-veg-udiced.") And don't be a Fruit Snoot either—you know, people too snooty to eat fruit. I mean, consider the banana—what a deal! Grows on trees, delicious, good for you, and comes in its own handy zip-lock bag!

Now I know there's this big thing about how some people don't like vegetables. Of course, some people ADORE them. I swear, my wife is a vegetable nut. (Wait a minute—that's like calling somebody a "cereal meat.") She's practically like Peter Rabbit in the old story—I've gotta keep her from running into people's gardens and stuffing herself silly.

But see, I'm different. When I was still a young little Polite Dude, the only vegetable I could stand was corn. My wife, for instance, will say, "Dude, you're an awesome man—but you're wrong about beets. Beets can't be beat."

And I'll say, "Oh yes they can. You can dump 'em on the street and beat 'em with a stick, which is as close as I'll ever get to 'em."

And she actually LOVES Brussels sprouts, which I tend to think of as smelly organic ping-pong balls. (Hey, what do you know? Some ping-pong balls ARE edible!)

But what I'm trying to say is . . . be OPEN to vegetables as much as you can, and to all healthy food in general. Because a miracle occurred in my life: I started really liking a number of different vegetables! I still can't believe it!

I love some of them so much—well, let me give you an example. Remember that cool ancient Chinese guy Shu Hsi who wrote

that "Rhapsody" about noodles? Well, I wrote a rhapsody too—
and considering what a veg-prej kid I used to
be, you aren't gonna believe what I got rap-
turous about. Read on. (This poem is best
when you read it out loud; if the librarian
objects, tell her Rude Dude said to.)

MY VEGETABLE CONFESSION

Kids, I have to tell the truth:
I am no longer in my youth,
and maybe that is why, you see,
I can now eat—broccoli.

Most of you, I understand,
would rather bite a frying pan
than chomp down on this tree-like veg
tougher than a new-trimmed hedge,

and I was just the same, when I
was young like you, and veggie-shy,
but something happened as I grew—
and now I even LIKE to chew

on that sweet stalk which my Aunt Polly
fondly titles "brolly-colly."
I mean, it's weird—I used to hate it!
But just last night—yeah—I ate it.

I like it steamed, or dipped in cheese,
or in the food we call Chinese.
I even like the crunch. By golly,
I'm very fond of brolly-colly!

So, kids, don't be surprised to find
your taste buds changing over time—
for someday, just like me, you might
consider broc for din one night,

no longer fearful that you'll hurl,
say, "Heck—I'll give that stuff a whirl!"
You don't believe me? But it's true!
I used to hate it just like you!

And now I'm like some dinosaur,
chomping on the swamps of yore.
I'm getting weirder by the hour!
What's next? The scrumptious colly-flower?!

REMEMBER: The Dude cares about all you dudes! He thinks
U R 1-derful! So he wants you to watch what you eat, OK?

And if you do, you'll be healthier and smarter and happier, and
the world will be a better place!

And THAT'S the most Chicken 65 of all!

Happy eating!

Your bud,

RUDE DUDE

Quiz Answers

TO THE QUIZ FROM CHAPTER 2, "CHOC ROCKS":

Dudes, you really had to look this up? Come on! If you don't know the answer, go back and re-read the chapter. And I'll still be expecting those five boxcars' worth of peanut butter cups, by the way.

TO THE RIDDLE AT THE END OF CHAPTER 4, "OODLES OF—WHAT ELSE?":

Did you like my riddle, Braniac? Did you figure it out? It's chopsticks. See?

LESSON IDEAS FOR RUDE DUDE'S BOOK OF FOOD

The following unit ideas each operate at the highest Bloom's Taxonomy levels, meet many Common Core standards (see below), and are based on the Common Core principle of students interacting critically with rich, challenging texts. Each can be adapted for younger students.

1–FOOD HISTORY JIGSAW

Food history is a unique and motivating way to help students see broader historical forces and interactions (as well as many other things!). Using the question "Is food just something we eat?" as a jumping-off point, the teacher breaks the students into small cooperative-learning groups. Each group is responsible for one chapter in the book.

The task: "Let's pretend that an evil dictator says we're wasting our time by reading about food history, since food is just something we eat. Using your chapter, show that it's valuable to learn about food history. You can come up with any reasons you like, but you must back them up with evidence from the book (or from other research)."

It's often best to give each group member a particular job: discussion leader; note-taker; oral presenter (though there can be more than one); "on-tasker" (keeps everyone on task AND makes sure all members of the group are heard); and, very importantly, devil's advocate (who tries to make the main point stronger by bringing up opposing arguments).

The students will then present orally as groups, each group acting as one piece of the ultimate jigsaw puzzle. You could even have the students make an actual jigsaw puzzle as a visual organizer or aid for oral presentation.

After the jigsaw presentations, each student will write an essay defending the study of food history (or speaking against it); the group work and presentations will have provided the student with lots of support information and critical analysis for his or her essay.

2—Foods Analysis Unit

With childhood obesity and other food-related problems on the rise, it's important to be able to determine which foods and food habits are healthy. This unit combines science and research skills to help students make better food choices.

After an introduction or review of appropriate research strategies, the teacher breaks the students into small cooperative-learning groups. Each group is responsible for one chapter in the book and must research the health qualities of that particular food. One way of doing this would be to have students predict, before any research, how healthy or unhealthy that food is, then compare their predictions with what they find through research.

The results can then be shared with the class (or with other classes, even the whole school) in a variety of ways: oral presentation; PowerPoint; video; student-made or student-written website; blog; or visual work like posters. Students could also keep personal food logs to think critically about their own food habits.

The final assignment could be individual essays in which students discuss what they've learned and how they plan to apply it.

3—Food and Globalization

We live in a time when much is being shared, copied, etc., on a global scale. After reading about the global spread of popular foods, student groups can research other things or ideas that are being spread globally. Possibilities include music, movies, TV shows, fashion, ideas, forms of government, words or ways of speaking/languages, inventions, stories, fads, etc. (Research could determine other options.)

Student groups could then each choose some idea, object, etc., that has spread around the world and research it, sharing their findings with the class. (One way to present this might be through skits.)

The climax of the unit comes when students divide into debate groups and debate the pros and cons of globalization. Individual student essays could follow.

How Rude Dude's Book of Food Meets Common Core Standards

According to the National Governors Association and the Council of Chief State School Officers (www.corestandards.org), "Students who are College and Career ready . . . come to understand other perspectives and cultures . . . and . . . acquire the habits of reading independently." They are able to "describe the connection between a series of historical events . . . or concepts." The principles of rich multicultural and historical knowledge is at the heart of the Common Core—and of *Rude Dude's Book of Food*.

But the book also meets many of the Core's English and Social Studies/History Standards for 3rd through 6th grade (and can be adapted to, for example, science objectives or research objectives; see above). It also clearly fits with the general reading standards, especially since it's highly motivating and rich in vocabulary and expression. And it can easily be used as a jumping-off point for many Common Core writing standards.

(I've eliminated any standards that are repeated across the grade levels or under different headings, so there are actually many more than appear here.)

Social Studies/History
(Retrieved 6/27/13 from http://www.corestandards.org/assets/CCSSI_ELA%20 Standards.pdf)

GENERAL:

Students who are college and career ready in reading, writing, speaking, listening, and language:

- build strong content knowledge
- establish a base of knowledge across a wide range of subject matter by engaging with works of quality and substance . . . to gain both general knowledge and discipline-specific expertise
- know that different disciplines call for different types of evidence (e.g., documentary evidence in history)
- come to understand other perspectives and cultures . . . through reading
- evaluate other points of view critically and constructively. Through reading . . . students can vicariously inhabit worlds and have experiences much different than their own

K—5 STANDARDS:

3. Analyze how and why individuals, events, [and]. . . ideas develop and interact over the course of a text

10. Read and comprehend complex literary and informational texts . . . proficiently

GRADE 3:

4. Determine the meaning of words and phrases as they are used in a text, distinguishing literal from non-literal language . . . including figurative language such as metaphors and similes

5. Explain how a series of chapters, scenes, or stanzas fits together to provide the overall structure of a particular story

K—5 INFORMATIONAL TEXT STANDARDS:

3. Describe the connection between a series of historical events . . . or concepts . . . in a text

8. Describe how reasons support specific points the author makes in a text

GRADE 3:

3. Describe the relationship between a series of historical events . . . using language that pertains to time, sequence, and cause/effect

4. Determine the meaning of general academic and domain-specific words and phrases in a text relevant to a Grade 3 topic or subject area

5. Use text features and search tools (e.g., sidebars) to locate information

8. Describe the logical connection between particular sentences and paragraphs in a text

GRADE 4:

2. Determine the main idea of a text and explain how it is supported by key details; summarize

5. Describe the overall structure . . . of events, ideas, concepts, or information in a text

GRADE 5:

—Determine two or more main ideas of a text and explain how they are supported by key details; summarize the text

5. Compare and contrast the overall structure . . . of events,

ideas, concepts, or information in two or more texts

College and Career Readiness Anchor Standards for Language

3. Apply knowledge of language to understand how language functions in different contexts . . . and to comprehend more fully when reading

4. Determine or clarify the meaning of unknown and multiple-meaning words and phrases by using context clues, analyzing meaningful word parts, and consulting general and specialized reference materials, as appropriate

5. Demonstrate understanding of . . . nuances in word meanings

GRADE 3:

b. Recognize and observe differences between the conventions of spoken and written standard English

b. Identify real-life connections between words and their use

c. Distinguish shades of meaning among related words

GRADE 4:

b. Recognize and explain the meaning of common idioms, adages, and proverbs

STANDARD 10: RANGE, QUALITY, AND COMPLEXITY OF STUDENT READING K–5

- Qualitative evaluation of the text: Levels of meaning, structure, language conventionality and clarity, and knowledge demands

- Matching reader to text and task: Reader variables (such as motivation, knowledge, and experiences) and task variables (such as purpose and the complexity generated by the task assigned and the questions posed)
- Informational text: Includes . . . books about history, social studies

COLLEGE AND CAREER READINESS ANCHOR STANDARDS FOR READING 6–12:

"Through wide and deep reading of literature and literary nonfiction of steadily increasing sophistication, students gain a reservoir of literary and cultural knowledge, references, and images; the ability to evaluate intricate arguments; and the capacity to surmount the challenges posed by complex texts."

KEY IDEAS AND DETAILS

1. Read closely to determine what the text says explicitly and to make logical inferences from it

2. Determine central ideas or themes of a text and analyze their development

3. Analyze how and why individuals, events, and ideas develop and interact over the course of a text

CRAFT AND STRUCTURE

4. Interpret words and phrases as they are used in a text . . . and analyze how specific word choices shape meaning or tone

5. Analyze the structure of texts, including how specific sentences, paragraphs, and larger portions of the text (e.g., a section,

chapter, scene, or stanza) relate to each other and the whole

6. Assess how point of view or purpose shapes the content and style of a text

GRADE 6:

2. Determine a theme or central idea of a text and how it is conveyed through particular details; provide a summary of the text distinct from personal opinions or judgments

READING STANDARDS FOR INFORMATIONAL TEXT 6—12

GRADE 6:

2. Determine a central idea of a text and how it is conveyed through particular details; provide a summary of the text distinct from personal opinions or judgments

3. Analyze in detail how a key individual, event, or idea is introduced, illustrated, and elaborated in a text (e.g., through examples or anecdotes)

6. Determine an author's point of view or purpose in a text and explain how it is conveyed in the text

LANGUAGE STANDARDS 6—12

GRADE 6:

a. Vary sentence patterns for meaning, reader / listener interest, and style

b. Maintain consistency in style and tone

c. Distinguish among the connotations (associations) of words with similar denotations (definitions)

3. Apply knowledge of language to understand how language functions in different contexts, to make effective choices for meaning or style, and to comprehend more fully when reading or listening

RANGE OF TEXT TYPES FOR 6—12

"Literary nonfiction: Includes the subgenres of exposition, argument, and functional text in the form of historical . . . accounts . . . written for a broad audience."

RANGE OF READING AND LEVEL OF TEXT COMPLEXITY

"Reading is critical to building knowledge in history / social studies . . . and the capacity to evaluate intricate arguments, synthesize complex information, and follow detailed descriptions of events and concepts . . . because the vast majority of reading in college and workforce training programs will be sophisticated nonfiction."

About the Author

Tim J. Myers is a writer, storyteller, songwriter, and teacher. He has eleven children's books out and three on the way, has won numerous awards, and has published fiction, non-fiction, and poetry for children and adults.

He lives in Santa Clara, California, is the oldest of eleven children, and can whistle and hum at the same time—though he hasn't won any awards for that . . . yet.

About Familius

Welcome to a place where mothers are celebrated, not compared. Where heart is at the center of our families, and family at the center of our homes. Where boo boos are still kissed, cake beaters are still licked, and mistakes are still okay. Welcome to a place where books—and family— are beautiful. Familius: a book publisher dedicated to helping families be happy.

Visit Our Website: www.familius.com

Our website is a different kind of place. Get inspired, read articles, discover books, watch videos, connect with our family experts, download books and apps and audiobooks, and along the way, discover how values and happy family life go together.

Join Our Family

There are lots of ways to connect with us! Subscribe to our newsletters at www.familius.com to receive uplifting daily inspiration, essays from our Pater Familius, a free ebook every month, and the first word on special discounts and Familius news.

Become an Expert

Familius authors and other established writers interested in helping families be happy are invited to join our family and contribute online content. If you have something important to say on the family, join our expert community by applying at:

www.familius.com/apply-to-become-a-familius-expert

Get Bulk Discounts

If you feel a few friends and family might benefit from what you've read, let us know and we'll be happy to provide you with quantity discounts. Simply email us at specialorders@familius.com.

Website: www.familius.com

Facebook: www.facebook.com/paterfamilius

Twitter: @familiustalk, @paterfamilius1

Pinterest: www.pinterest.com/familius

The most important work

you ever do will be within the

walls of your own home.

CPSIA information can be obtained at www.ICGtesting.com
Printed in the USA
BVOW07s0708080814

361821BV00002B/2/P